Holt California Algebra 1

Know-It Notebook™

HOLT, RINEHART AND WINSTON

A Harcourt Education Company

Orlando • **Austin** • New York • San Diego • London

ISBN-13: 978-0-030-94680-6
ISBN-10: 0-03-094680-8

7 8 9   862   10 09 08

Contents

Algebra 1

USING THE *KNOW-IT NOTEBOOK*™

This *Know-It Notebook* will help you take notes, organize your thinking, and study for quizzes and tests. There are *Know-It Notes*™ pages for every lesson in your textbook. These notes will help you identify important mathematical information that you will need later.

Know-It Notes
Vocabulary

One good note-taking practice is to keep a list of important vocabulary.

- Use the page references or the glossary in your textbook to find each definition and a clarifying example.
- Write each definition and example on the lines provided.

Lesson Objectives

Another good note-taking practice is to know the objectives that each lesson covers.

Key Concepts

Key concepts from each lesson are included. The graphic organizers from the Think and Discuss questions at the end of each lesson are also included. These are indicated in your student book with the Know-it Note! logo.

- Write each answer in the space provided.
- Check your answers with your book.
- Ask your teacher to help you with any concept that you don't understand.

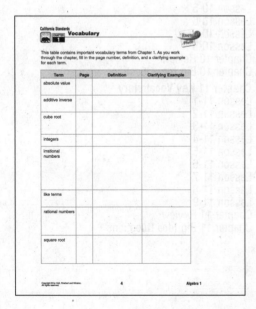

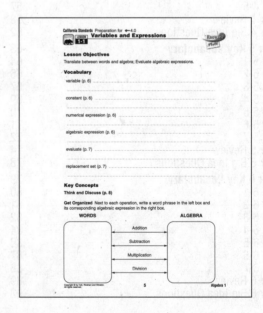

Algebra 1

Chapter Review

Complete Chapter Review problems for each lesson. This is a good review before you take the chapter test.

- Write each answer in the space provided.
- Check your answers with your teacher or another student.
- Ask your teacher to help you understand any problem that you answered incorrectly.

Big Ideas

The Big Ideas have you summarize the important chapter concepts in your own words. Putting ideas in your words requires that you think about the ideas and understand them. This will also help you remember them.

- Write each answer in the space provided.
- Check your answers with your teacher or another student.
- Ask your teacher to help you understand any question that you answered incorrectly.

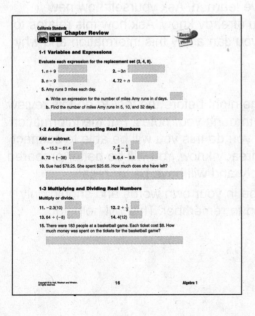

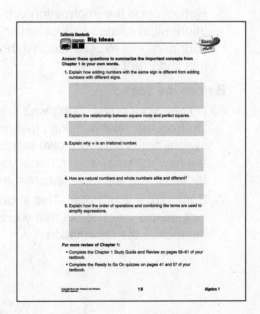

1

Algebra 1

NOTE TAKING STRATEGIES

Taking good notes is very important in many of your classes and will be even more important when you take college classes. This Notebook was designed to help you get started. Here are some other steps that can help you take good notes.

Getting Ready

1. Use a loose-leaf notebook. You can add pages to this where and when you want to. It will help keep you organized.

During the Lecture

2. If you are taking notes during a lecture, write the big ideas. Use abbreviations to save time. Do not worry about spelling or writing every word. Use headings to show changes in the topics discussed. Use numbering or bullets to organize supporting ideas under each topic heading. Leave space before each new heading so that you can fill in more information later.

After the Lecture

3. As soon as possible after the lecture, read through your notes and add any information you can so that when you review your notes later, they make sense. You should also summarize the information into key words or key phrases. This will help your comprehension and will help you process the information. These key words and key phrases will be your memory cues when you are reviewing or taking a test. At this time you may also want to write questions to help clarify the meaning of the ideas and facts.

4. Read your notes out loud. As you do this, state the ideas in your own words and do as much as you can by memory. This will help you remember and will also help with your thinking process. It helps you think about and understand the information.

5. Reflect upon the information you have learned. Ask yourself how new information relates to information you already know. Ask how this relates to your personal experience. Ask how you can apply this information and why it is important.

Before the Test

6. Review your notes. Don't wait until the night before the test to do this review. Do frequent reviews. Don't just read through your notes. Put the information in your notes into your own words. If you do this you will be able to connect the new material with material you already know. You will be better prepared for tests. You will have less test anxiety and will have better recall.

7. Summarize your notes. This should be in your own words and should only include the main points that you need to remember. This will help you internalize the information.

Algebra 1

Algebra 1

Vocabulary

This table contains important vocabulary terms from Chapter 1. As you work through the chapter, fill in the page number, definition, and a clarifying example for each term.

Term	Page	Definition	Clarifying Example
absolute value			
additive inverse			
cube root			
integers			
irrational numbers			
like terms			
rational numbers			
square root			

Algebra 1

Variables and Expressions

LESSON 1-1

Lesson Objectives

Translate between words and algebra; Evaluate algebraic expressions.

Vocabulary

variable (p. 6) _____

_____

constant (p. 6) _____

_____

numerical expression (p. 6) _____

_____

algebraic expression (p. 6) _____

_____

evaluate (p. 7) _____

_____

replacement set (p. 7) _____

_____

Key Concepts

Think and Discuss (p. 8)

Get Organized Next to each operation, write a word phrase in the left box and its corresponding algebraic expression in the right box.

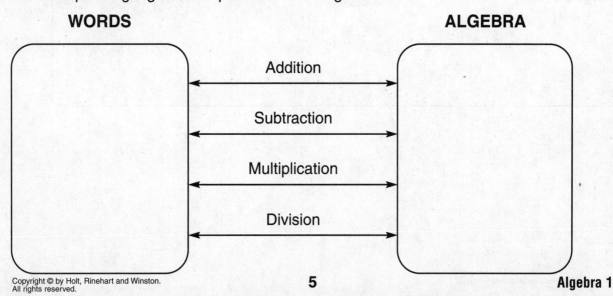

WORDS | ALGEBRA
Addition
Subtraction
Multiplication
Division

Algebra 1

LESSON 1-2
Adding and Subtracting Real Numbers

Know it!
Note

Lesson Objectives

Add real numbers; Subtract real numbers

Vocabulary

real numbers (p. 14) _____

_____

absolute value (p. 14) _____

_____

opposites (p. 15) _____

_____

additive inverse (p. 15) _____

_____

Key Concepts

Adding Real Numbers (p. 15):

WORDS	NUMBERS
Adding Numbers with the Same Sign	
Adding Numbers with Different Signs	

Algebra 1

Inverse Property of Addition (p. 15):

WORDS	NUMBERS	ALGEBRA

Subtracting Real Numbers (p. 15):

WORDS	NUMBERS	ALGEBRA

Think and Discuss (p. 17)

Get Organized For each pair of points, tell whether the sum and the difference of the first point and the second point are positive or negative.

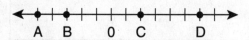

POINTS	SUM	DIFFERENCE
A, B		
B, A		
C, B		
D, A		

Algebra 1

LESSON 1-3 Multiplying and Dividing Real Numbers

Lesson Objectives

Multiply real numbers; Divide real numbers

Vocabulary

reciprocal (p. 21) _____

_____

multiplicative inverse (p. 21) _____

_____

Key Concepts

Multiplying and Dividing Real Numbers (p. 20):

WORDS	NUMBERS
Multiplying and Dividing Numbers with the Same Sign	
Multiplying and Dividing Number with Different Signs	

Inverse Property of Multiplication (p. 21):

WORDS	NUMBERS	ALGEBRA

Algebra 1

Properties of Zero (p. 21):

WORDS	NUMBERS	ALGEBRA
Multiplication by Zero		
Zero Divided by a Number		
Division by Zero		

Think and Discuss (p. 22)

Get Organized In each blank, write "pos" or "neg" to indicate positive or negative.

Multiplying and Dividing Numbers

MULTIPLICATION		DIVISION	
pos ×	= **pos**	**pos** ÷	= **pos**
pos ×	= **neg**	**pos** ÷	= **neg**
neg ×	= **neg**	**neg** ÷	= **neg**
neg ×	= **pos**	**neg** ÷	= **pos**

Algebra 1

LESSON 1-4

Powers and Exponents

Lesson Objectives

Evalute expressions containing exponents

Vocabulary

power (p. 26) _____

_____

base (p. 26) _____

_____

exponent (p. 26) _____

_____

Key Concepts

Think and Discuss (p. 28)

Get Organized In each box, give an example and tell whether the expression is positive or negative.

	Even Exponent	Odd Exponent
Positive Base		
Negative Base		

Algebra 1

LESSON 1-5

Roots and Irrational Numbers

Lesson Objectives

Evaluate expressions containing roots; Classify numbers within the real number system

Vocabulary

square root (p. 32) _____

_____

principal square root (p. 32) _____

_____

perfect square (p. 32) _____

_____

cube root (p. 32) _____

_____

natural numbers (p. 33) _____

_____

whole numbers (p. 33) _____

_____

integers (p. 33) _____

_____

rational numbers (p. 33) _____

_____

terminating decimal (p. 33) _____

_____

repeating decimal (p. 33) _____

_____

irrational numbers (p. 34) _____

_____

11

Algebra 1

Key Concepts

Real Numbers (p. 34):

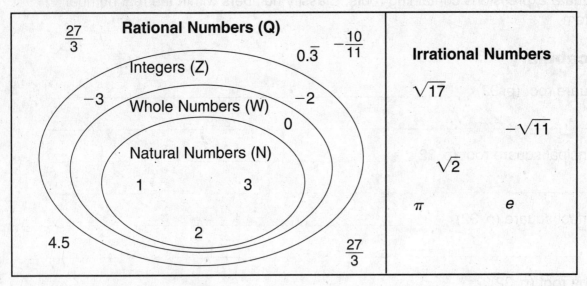

Think and Discuss (p. 35)

Get Organized Use the flowchart to classify each of the given numbers. Write each number in the box with the most specific classification that applies. 4, $\sqrt{25}$, 0, $\frac{1}{3}$, −15, −2.25, $\frac{1}{4}$, $\sqrt{21}$, 2^4, $(−1)^2$

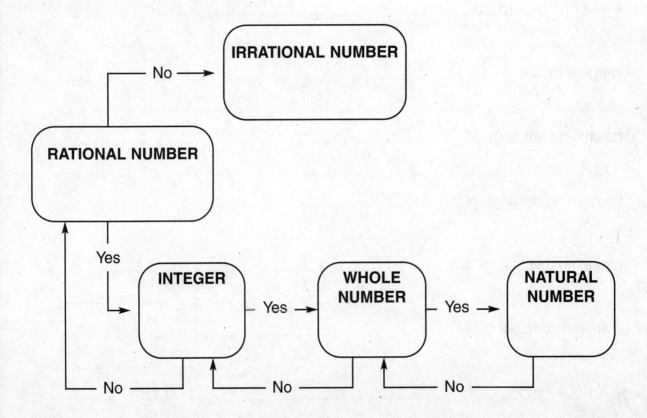

Algebra 1

Properties of Real Numbers

LESSON 1-6

Lesson Objectives

Use the order of operations to simplify expressions

Vocabulary

counterexample (p. 43) _____

_____

closure (p. 44) _____

_____

_____

Key Concepts

Properties of Addition and Multiplication (p. 42):

WORDS	NUMBERS	ALGEBRA
Commutative Property		
Associative Property		

Algebra 1

Distributive Property (p. 43):

NUMBERS	ALGEBRA

Closure Property of the Real Numbers (p. 43):

WORDS	NUMBERS	ALGEBRA

Think and Discuss (p. 45)

Get Organized In each box, give an example to illustrate the given property.

Simplifying Expressions

Lesson Objectives

Use the order of operations and properties of the real number system to simplify expressions; Combine like terms

Vocabulary

order of operations (p. 48) _____

_____

_____

_____

terms (p. 49) _____

_____

like terms (p. 49) _____

_____

coefficient (p. 49) _____

Key Concepts

Think and Discuss (p. 50)

Get Organized In each box, give an example of an expression that can be simplified using the given method. Then simplify your expressions.

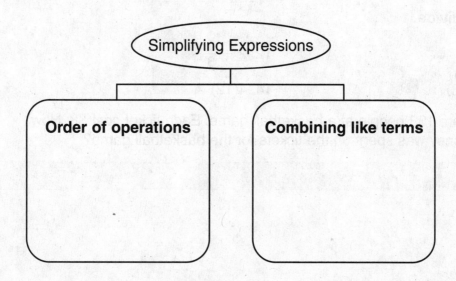

Algebra 1

Chapter Review

1-1 Variables and Expressions

Evaluate each expression for the replacement set {3, 4, 8}.

1. $n + 9$

2. $-3n$

3. $n - 9$

4. $72 \div n$

5. Amy runs 3 miles each day.

    a. Write an expression for the number of miles Amy runs in *d* days.

    b. Find the number of miles Amy runs in 5, 10, and 32 days.

1-2 Adding and Subtracting Real Numbers

Add or subtract.

6. $-15.3 - 61.4$

7. $\dfrac{4}{9} - \dfrac{1}{3}$

8. $72 + (-38)$

9. $6.4 - 9.8$

10. Sue had $78.25. She spent $25.65. How much does she have left?

1-3 Multiplying and Dividing Real Numbers

Multiply or divide.

11. $-2.3(10)$

12. $2 \div \dfrac{1}{3}$

13. $64 \div (-8)$

14. $4(12)$

15. There were 183 people at a basketball game. Each ticket cost $8. How much money was spent on the tickets for the basketball game?

Algebra 1

1-4 Powers and Exponents

Write each number as a power of the given base.

16. 16; base -2

17. 1024; base 4

18. 625; base 5

19. -27; base -3

20. A certain species started with two and doubled every day. How many species were there after 8 days?

1-5 Roots and Irrational Numbers

Find each root.

21. $\sqrt{121}$

22. $\sqrt[3]{-216}$

23. $\sqrt[3]{\dfrac{27}{64}}$

24. $\sqrt{\dfrac{9}{25}}$

25. Brian's square pool has an area of 124 ft². Estimate the side length of his pool.

Write all classifications that apply to each real number.

26. $.\sqrt{15}$

27. -7.2

28. $\sqrt{64}$

1-6 Properties of Real Numbers

Name the property that is illustrated in each equation.

29. $3 + (7 + 6x) = (3 + 7) + 6x$

30. $x \cdot (-5) = -5x$

Write each product using the Distributive Property. Then simplify.

31. 5(47)

32. 12(104)

33. Find a counterexample to show that the statement is false: The set of negative integers is closed under subtraction.

Algebra 1

1-7 Simplifying Expressions

Simplify each expression.

34. $-35 + \sqrt{12 \div 3}$

35. $(6 + 3 \cdot 2) \div (8 - 6)^2$

36. $\dfrac{0 - 18}{6 \div 2}$

37. $\dfrac{4 + 6(6)}{2^2}$

Simplify each expression by combining like terms.

38. $8x - 2 + 4x$

39. $-12p + 15p$

40. $6(5 - y) + 5y$

41. $a - 5(2a + a^2)$

42. The volume of a cylindrical container can be found using $\pi r^2(h)$. Find the volume of a container with $r = 3$ inches and $h = 8$ inches. (Use 3.14 for π.)

Algebra 1

Answer these questions to summarize the important concepts from Chapter 1 in your own words.

1. Explain how adding numbers with the same sign is different from adding numbers with different signs.

2. Explain the relationship between square roots and perfect squares.

3. Explain why π is an irrational number.

4. How are natural numbers and whole numbers alike and different?

5. Explain how the order of operations and combining like terms are used to simplify expressions.

For more review of Chapter 1:

• Complete the Chapter 1 Study Guide and Review on pages 58–61 of your textbook.

• Complete the Ready to Go On quizzes on pages 41 and 57 of your textbook.

Algebra 1

Vocabulary

The table contains important vocabulary terms from Chapter 2. As you work through the chapter, fill in the page number, definition, and a clarifying example.

Term	Page	Definition	Clarifying Example
cross products			
deductive reasoning			
equation			
proportion			
rate			
ratio			
scale			
scale drawing			
scale model			
solution set			
unit rate			

Algebra 1

LESSON 2-1 Solving One-Step Equations

Lesson Objectives

Solve one-step equations in one variable

Vocabulary

equation (p. 72) _____

_____

solution of an equation (p. 72) _____

_____

solution set (p. 72) _____

_____

Key Concepts

Addition and Subtraction Properties of Equality (p. 72):

WORDS	NUMBERS	ALGEBRA
Addition Property of Equality		
Subtraction Property of Equality		

21

Algebra 1

Multiplication and Division Properties of Equality (p. 73):

WORDS	NUMBERS	ALGEBRA
Multiplication Property of Equality		
Division Property of Equality		

Think and Discuss (p. 75)

Get Organized In each box, write an example of an equation that can be solved by using the given property, and solve it.

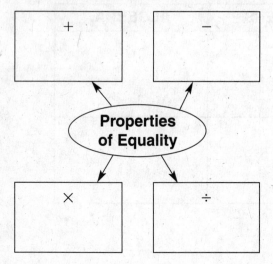

LESSON 2-2 Solving Two-Step Equations

Lesson Objectives

Solve two-step equations in one variable

Vocabulary

equivalent equations (p. 79) _____

_____

Key Concepts

Think and Discuss (p. 82)

Get Organized In each box, write and solve a two-step equation. Use addition, subtraction, multiplication, and division at least one time each.

Solving Two-Step Equations	

Algebra 1

LESSON 2-3 Solving Multi-Step Equations

Lesson Objectives

Solve equations in one variable that contain more than one operation

Key Concepts

Think and Discuss (p. 87)

Get Organized In each box, write and solve a multi-step equation. Use addition, subtraction, multiplication, and division at least one time each.

Solving Multi-Step Equations	

24

Algebra 1

LESSON 2-4 Solving Equations with Variables on Both Sides

Lesson Objectives

Solve equations in one variable that contain variable terms on both sides

Vocabulary

identity (p. 93): _____

_____

Key Concepts

Think and Discuss (p. 95)

Get Organized In each box, write an equation that has the indicated number of solutions.

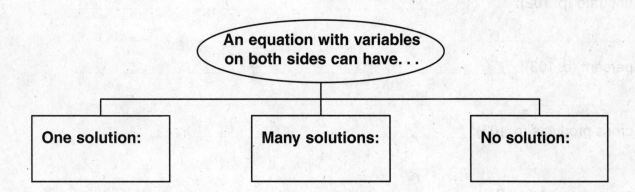

An equation with variables on both sides can have. . .

| One solution: | Many solutions: | No solution: |

Algebra 1

Solving Proportions

Lesson Objectives

Write and use ratios, rates, and unit rates; Write and solve proportions

Vocabulary

ratio (p. 102): _____

_____

proportion (p. 102): _____

_____

rate (p. 102): _____

_____

unit rate (p. 102): _____

_____

percent (p. 103): _____

_____

cross products (p. 103): _____

_____

scale drawing (p. 104): _____

_____

scale (p. 104): _____

_____

scale model (p. 104): _____

_____

Algebra 1

Key Concepts

Cross Products Property (p. 103):

WORDS	NUMBERS	ALGEBRA

Think and Discuss (p. 104)

Get Organized In each box, write an example of each use of ratios.

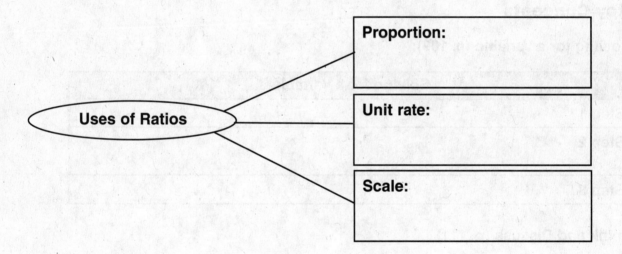

Uses of Ratios

Proportion:

Unit rate:

Scale:

Algebra 1

Solving Literal Equations for a Variable

Lesson Objectives

Solve a formula for a given variable; Solve an equation in two or more variables for one of the variables

Vocabulary

formula (p. 109): _____

_____

literal equation (p. 110): _____

_____

Key Concepts

Solving for a Variable (p. 109):

Solving for a Variable
Step 1
Step 2
Step 3

Think and Discuss (p. 111)

Get Organized Write a formula that is used in each subject. Then solve the formula for each of its variables.

Common Formulas	
Subject	**Formula**
Geometry	
Physical science	
Earth science	

Algebra 1

Solving Absolute-Value Equations

Lesson Objectives

Solve equations in one variable that contain absolute-value expressions

Key Concepts

Absolute-Value Equations (p. 114):

WORDS	NUMBERS
GRAPH	**ALGEBRA**

Solving an Absolute-Value Equation (p. 115):

Solving an Absolute-Value Equation
1.
2.
3.

Think and Discuss (p. 116)

Get Organized In each box, write an example of an absolute-value equation that has the indicated number of solutions, and then solve.

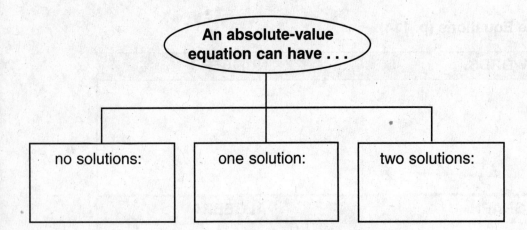

An absolute-value equation can have . . .

| no solutions: | one solution: | two solutions: |

Algebra 1

Chapter Review

2-1 Solving One-Step Equations

Solve each equation.

1. $a + 45 = 36$ **2.** $5 - b = 0.65$ **3.** $5a = 25$ **4.** $-\frac{1}{3}c = -\frac{2}{3}$

5. Gary had $231. After he bought a video game, he had $186. Write and solve an equation to find the amount of money Gary spent on the video game.

2-2 Solving Two-Step Equations

Solve each equation.

6. $-2a + 8 = 14$ **7.** $8.5b - 6 = 53.5$ **8.** $9 - \frac{1}{4}c = \frac{3}{8}$ **9.** $5d + 24 = -36$

10. A car can be rented for $45 plus $0.14 per mile. Tammy paid $63.90. Write and solve an equation to show how many miles Tammy drove.

2-3 Solving Multi-Step Equations

Solve each equation. Check your answer.

11. $\frac{d + 7}{4} = 3$ **12.** $5h - 7 + h = 5$

13. $3(p - 2) = 18$ **14.** $\frac{9k - 7}{4} = 5$

15. Marty organized his CDs onto 4 shelves. The top shelf holds 3 CDs, the second shelf holds 6, and the 2 bottom shelves hold the same number of CDs. Marty has a total of 19 CDs. How many CDs does the bottom shelf hold?

Algebra 1

2-4 Solving Equations with Variables on Both Sides

Solve each equation. Check your answer.

16. $a + 15 = -4a$ **17.** $0.45b = 2.25b - 9$ **18.** $\frac{3}{5}c - \frac{1}{5} = \frac{1}{10}c$ **19.** $-2d - 14 = -4 + d$

2-5 Solving Proportions

Solve each proportion.

20. $\frac{6}{d} = \frac{2}{16}$ **21.** $\frac{t}{5} = \frac{25}{20}$ **22.** $\frac{0.5}{1.5} = \frac{2.5}{m - 0.5}$

23. A hummingbird's heart beats 1263 beats per minute. Find the unit rate in beats per second. Round to the nearest hundredth.

2-6 Solving Literal Equations for a Variable

24. Solve $p = 4 - m$ for m.

25. Solve $ab = 8 - c$ for a.

26. Solve $mn - 3 = s$ for n.

27. Solve $\frac{d - 5}{f} = g$ for f.

28. The formula for the perimeter of a rectangle is $P = 2l + 2w$, where l is the length and w is the width. Solve for w.

2-7 Solving Absolute-Value Equations

Solve each equation.

29. $9 = |x + 4|$

30. $5|x + 5| + 10 = 7$

31. $|x - 3| - 8 = 2$

32. $|x - 50.37| = 22.07$

33. In the winter Bruce keeps his room thermostat set at 67°F to conserve energy. The thermostat controls the furnace so that the room temperature stays within 3° of this setting. Write and solve an equation to find the minimum and maximum temperatures in the Bruce's room.

Algebra 1

Answer these questions to summarize the important concepts from Chapter 2 in your own words.

1. Explain how the four properties of equality help you solve equations.

2. Explain how you can solve a proportion for a missing value.

3. What are the steps for solving a literal equation for a variable?

4. Explain why an absolute-value equation may not have two solutions.

For more review of Chapter 2:

- Complete the Chapter 2 Study Guide and Review on pages 122–125 of your textbook.

- Complete the Ready to Go On quizzes on pages 101 and 121 of your textbook.

Algebra 1

Vocabulary

The table contains important vocabulary terms from Chapter 3. As you work through the chapter, fill in the page number, definition, and a clarifying example for each term.

Term	Page	Definition	Clarifying Example
compound inequality			
equivalent inequalities			
inequality			
intersection			
solution of an inequality			
union			

Algebra 1

 **LESSON 3-1**
Graphing and Writing Inequalities

Lesson Objectives

Identify solutions of inequalities in one variable; Write and graph inequalities in one variable

Vocabulary

inequality (p. 136) _____

_____

solution of an inequality (p. 136): _____

_____

Key Concepts

Graphing Inequalities (p. 137):

WORDS	ALGEBRA	GRAPH
All real numbers less than 5		-4 -3 -2 -1 0 1 2 3 4 5 6
All real numbers greater than −1		-4 -3 -2 -1 0 1 2 3 4 5 6
All real numbers less than or equal to $\frac{1}{2}$		-2 $-1\frac{1}{2}$ -1 $-\frac{1}{2}$ 0 $\frac{1}{2}$ 1
All real numbers greater than or equal to 0		-4 -3 -2 -1 0 1 2 3 4 5 6

Think and Discuss (p. 138)

Get Organized Draw a graph in the first row and write the correct inequality in the second row.

Inequality	Graph
$x > 1$	
	-5 -4 -3 -2 -1 0 1

Algebra 1

LESSON 3-2 Solving Inequalities by Adding or Subtracting

Lesson Objectives

Solve one-step inequalities by using addition; Solve one-step inequalities by using subtraction

Vocabulary

equivalent inequalities (p. 142): _____

_____

Key Concepts

Properties of Inequality (p. 142):

Addition and Subtraction		
WORDS	**NUMBERS**	**ALGEBRA**
Addition		
Subtraction		
These properties are also true for inequalities that use the symbols >, ≥, and ≤.		

Think and Discuss (p. 145)

Get Organized In each box, write an inequality that must use the specified property to solve. Then solve and graph your inequality.

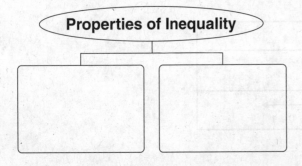

36

Algebra 1

LESSON 3-3

Solving Inequalities by Multiplying or Dividing

Lesson Objectives

Solve one-step inequalities by using multiplication; Solve one-step inequalities by using division

Key Concepts

Properties of inequality (p. 148):

Multiplication and Division by Positive Numbers		
WORDS	**NUMBERS**	**ALGEBRA**
Multiplication		
Division		
These properties are also true for inequalities that use the symbols >, ≥, and ≤.		

Properties of Inequality (p. 149):

Multiplication and Division by Negative Numbers		
WORDS	**NUMBERS**	**ALGEBRA**
Multiplication	$8 > 4$ $8(-2) < 4(-2)$ $-16 < -8$	
Division	$12 > 4$ $\dfrac{12}{-4} < \dfrac{4}{-4}$ $-3 < -1$	
These properties are also true for inequalities that use the symbols $>$, $\geq$, and $\leq$.		

Think and Discuss (p. 150)

Get Organized In each cell, write and solve an inequality.

Solving Inequalities by Using Multiplication and Division		
	By a Positive Number	**By a Negative Number**
Divide		
Multiply		

Algebra 1

LESSON 3-4 # Solving Two-Step and Multi-Step Inequalities

Lesson Objectives

Solve inequalities that contain more than one operation

Key Concepts

Think and Discuss (p. 158)

Get Organized Complete the graphic organizer.

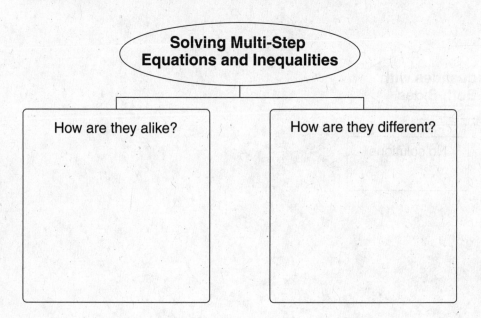

Solving Multi-Step Equations and Inequalities

How are they alike?

How are they different?

Algebra 1

Solving Inequalities with Variables on Both Sides

LESSON 3-5

Know it!
Note

Lesson Objectives

Solve inequalities that contain variable terms on both sides

Key Concepts

Think and Discuss (p. 165)

Get Organized In each box, give an example of an inequality of the indicated type.

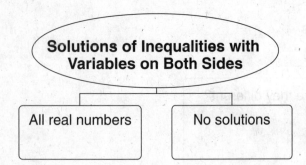

Solutions of Inequalities with Variables on Both Sides

| All real numbers | No solutions |

Algebra 1

Solving Compound Inequalities

LESSON
3-6

Lesson Objectives

Solve compound inequalities in one variable; Graph solution sets of compound inequalities in one variable

Vocabulary

compound inequality (p. 170): _____

_____

intersection (p. 171): _____

_____

union (p. 172): _____

_____

Key Concepts

Compound Inequalities (p. 170):

WORDS	ALGEBRA	GRAPH
All real numbers greater than 2 AND less than 6		
All real numbers greater than or equal to 2 AND less than or equal to 6		
All real numbers less than 2 OR greater than 6		
All real numbers less than or equal to 2 OR greater than or equal to 6		

Algebra 1

Think and Discuss (p. 173)

Get Organized Write three solutions in each of the three sections of the diagram. Then write each of your nine solutions in the appropriate column or columns of the table.

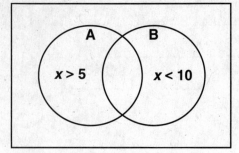

$x > 5$ AND $x < 10$	$x > 5$ OR $x < 10$

Algebra 1

LESSON
3-7
Solving Absolute-Value Inequalities

Lesson Objectives

Solve inequalities in one variable involving absolute-value expressions

Key Concepts

Absolute-Value inequalities Involving < (p. 178)

Absolute-Value Inequalities Involving <	
WORDS	**NUMBERS**
GRAPH	**ALGEBRA**
The same properties are true for inequalities that use the symbol ≤.	

Absolute Value Inequalities Involving > (p. 179)

Absolute-Value Inequalities Involving >	
WORDS	**NUMBERS**
GRAPH	**ALGEBRA**
The same properties are true for inequalities that use the symbol ≥.	

Algebra 1

Think and Discuss (p. 181)

Get Organized In each box, write an example of the indicated type of absolute-value inequality and then solve it.

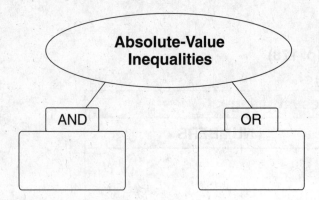

Algebra 1

3-1 Graphing and Writing Inequalities

Write the inequality shown by each graph.

1. ← (graph with closed dot at −5, arrow right) -4 -2 0 2 4

2. ← (graph with open circle at 2) -4 -2 0 2 4

3. ← (graph with closed dot at 0) -4 -2 0 2 4

Graph each inequality.

4. $r \geq -1$

5. $g < 2^2$

3-2 Solving Inequalities by Adding and Subtracting

Solve each inequality and graph the solutions.

6. $4 \geq t - 3$

7. $r + 7 < 12$

8. Danny must have at least 410 points to receive an A. He has 275 points. Write and solve an inequality to show the least number of points Danny needs to receive an A.

Algebra 1

3-3 Solving Inequalities by Multiplying and Dividing

Solve each inequality and graph the solutions.

9. $\frac{k}{3} \leq 2$

10. $3 > \frac{h}{-2}$

11. $-2r < -6$

12. Hannah wants to buy 4 presents for at least $60. She wants to spend an equal amount of money on each present. Write and solve an inequality to show the least amount of money Hannah will spend on each present.

3-4 Solving Two-Step and Multi-Step Inequalities

Solve each inequality.

13. $c + 3c > 2 + 14$

14. $2^3 + 12 \leq 2r - 12r$

15. $14 < \frac{6 - 2f}{2}$

16. $\frac{1}{3}b - \frac{1}{2} \geq \frac{5}{6}$

Solve each inequality and graph the solutions.

17. $-5a + 2 \geq 22$

18. $13 < 2t - 3(t - 3)$

Algebra 1

3-5 Solving Inequalities with Variables on Both Sides

Solve each inequality.

19. $\frac{1}{2}(3 - 8t) > 20(1 - \frac{1}{5}t)$

20. $2(4 - a) - 2 \leq -2a + 6$

Solve each inequality and graph the solutions.

21. $4(3m - 1) \geq 2(m + 3)$

22. $9d - 4 \geq 12 + 5d$

23. The booster club raised $104 to buy soccer balls for the soccer team. Each soccer ball costs $19. How many soccer balls can the booster club buy?

3-6 Solving Compound Inequalities

Solve each compound inequality and graph the solutions.

24. $-4 < r - 5 \leq -1$

25. $4v + 3 < -5$ or $-2v + 7 < 1$

Write the compound inequality shown by each graph.

26.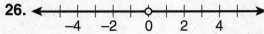

27.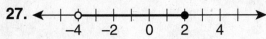

Algebra 1

3-7 Solving Absolute-Value Inequalities

Solve each inequality.

28. $|x| - 3 \leq -5$

29. $|3a| + 9 > 2$

Solve each absolute-value inequality and graph the solutions.

30. $|x + 3| \geq 2$

31. $|x + 2| - 2.8 < 3.2$

Write an absolute-value inequality for each graph.

32.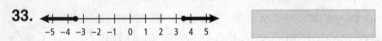

33.

Tell whether the given value of *x* is a solution of the inequality.

34. $|x| > 4; x = -6$

Answer these questions to summarize the important concepts from Chapter 3 in your own words.

1. Explain how to show that an endpoint is a solution. Explain how to show that an endpoint is not a solution.

2. Explain how solving a one-step or multi-step inequality is like solving a one-step or multi-step equation.

3. Explain how solving inequalities by multiplying or dividing by a negative number is different from solving inequalities by multiplying or dividing by a positive number.

4. Explain how to graph a compound inequality involving a union

5. Describe how to use an absolute-value inequality to find all the values on a number line that are within 3 units of -1.

For more review of Chapter 3:

- Complete the Chapter 3 Study Guide and Review on pages 186–189 of your textbook.

- Complete the Ready to Go On quizzes on pages 155 and 185 of your textbook.

Algebra 1

Vocabulary

This table contains important vocabulary terms from Chapter 4. As you work through the chapter, fill in the page number, definition, and a clarifying example for each term.

Term	Page	Definition	Clarifying Example
arithmetic sequence			
common difference			
correlation			
dependent variable			
domain			
function			
function notation			
independent variable			
range			
relation			

Algebra 1

LESSON
4-1

Graphing Relationships

Lesson Objectives

Match simple graphs with situations; Graph a relationship

Vocabulary

continuous graph (p. 201): _____

_____

discrete graph (p. 201): _____

_____

Key Concepts

Think and Discuss (p. 202)

Get Organized Write an example of key words that suggest the given segments on a graph. One example of each segment is given for you.

```
        ( Key Words for Graph Segments )
       _____|_____|_____
      |                 |                   |
  ┌─────────┐     ┌─────────┐         ┌─────────┐
  │   ╱     │     │   ╲     │         │  ────   │
  │         │     │         │         │         │
  │Increases│     │Decreases│         │Stays the│
  │         │     │         │         │  same   │
  └─────────┘     └─────────┘         └─────────┘
```

Algebra 1

Relations and Functions

Lesson Objectives

Identify functions; Find the domain and range of relations and functions

Vocabulary

relation (p. 206): _____

_____

domain (p. 206): _____

_____

range (p. 206): _____

_____

function (p. 207): _____

Key Concepts

Think and Discuss (p. 208)

Get Organized Explain when a relation is a function and when it is not a function.

A relation is...	
A function if...	Not a function if...

Algebra 1

Writing and Graphing Functions

LESSON 4-3

Lesson Objectives

Write an equation in function notation and evaluate a function for given input values; Graph functions and determine whether an equation represents a function.

Vocabulary

dependent variable (p. 216): _____

_____

independent variable (p. 216): _____

_____

function notation (p. 216): _____

_____

Key Concepts

The Vertical-Line Test

WORDS	GRAPHS	
	Function	Not a Function

Algebra 1

Think and Discuss (p. 217)

Get Organized Use the equation $y = x + 3$ to complete the graphic organizer.

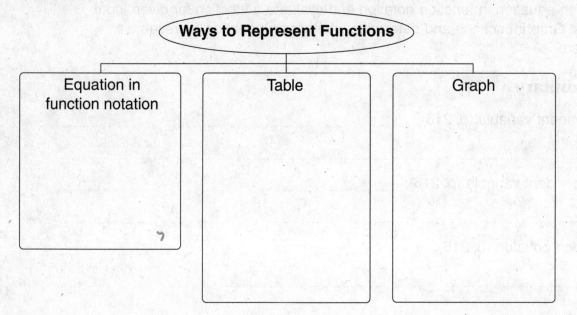

Ways to Represent Functions

| Equation in function notation | Table | Graph |

Scatter Plots and Trend Lines

Lesson Objectives

Create and interpret scatter plots; Use trend lines to make predictions

Vocabulary

scatter plot (p. 224): _____

_____

correlation (p. 224): _____

_____

positive correlation (p. 225): _____

_____

negative correlation (p. 225): _____

_____

no correlation (p. 225): _____

_____

trend line (p. 227): _____

_____

55

Algebra 1

Key Concepts

Correlations (p. 225):

Correlations		
Positive Correlation	**Negative Correlation**	**No Correlation**

Think and Discuss (p. 227)

Get Organized Complete the graphic organizer with either a scatter plot, or a real-world example, or both.

	GRAPH	EXAMPLE
Positive Correlation		
Negative Correlation		the amount of water in a watering can and the number of flowers watered
No Correlation		

Algebra 1

Arithmetic Sequences

Lesson Objectives

Recognize and extend an arithmetic sequence; Find a given term of an arithmetic sequence

Vocabulary

sequence (p. 234): _____

_____

term (p. 234): _____

_____

arithmetic sequence (p. 234): _____

_____

common difference (p. 234): _____

_____

Key Concepts

Finding the *n*th Term of an Arithmetic Sequence (p. 235):

Finding the *n*th Term of an Arithmetic Sequence

Think and Discuss (p. 236)

Get Organized Write steps for finding the *n*th term of an arithmetic sequence.

Finding the *n*th Term of an Arithmetic Sequence → 1. _____ → 2. _____

57   **Algebra 1**

Chapter Review

4-1 Graphing Relationships

Choose the graph that best represents each situation.

1. A person runs a marathon at a constant rate of speed.

2. A person jogs, slows down when approaching a crosswalk, stops for traffic, and then starts to jog again.

3. A person suddenly gets chased by a dog while jogging.

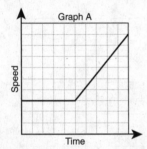

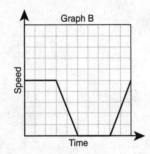

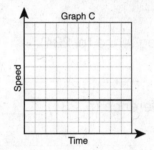

Write a possible situation for the graph.

4.

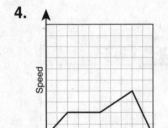

Algebra 1

4-2 Relations and Functions

Give the domain and range of each relation. Tell whether the relation is a function. Explain.

5.

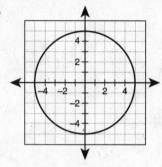

6. {(7, −7), (7, −7), (0, 0), (−7, 7), (−7, 7)}

4-3 Writing and Graphing Functions

Determine a relationship between the *x*- and *y*-values. Write an equation.

7.

x	1	2	3	4
y	0	2	4	6

8. {(2, −2), (4, −1), (6, 0), (8, 1)}

Identify the dependant and independent variables. Write a rule in function notation for the situation.

9. An Internet music web site charges $10 for a membership fee plus $0.99 for each song download.

Graph each equation. Then tell whether the equation represents a function.

10. $y = -\dfrac{1}{3}x - 1$

11. $y = |2x - 2|$

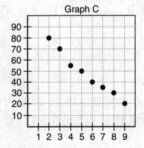

4-4 Scatter Plots and Trend Lines

Choose the scatter plot that best represents the described relationship. Explain.

12. mathematics test score and number of hours studying

13. mathematics test score and number of missed test questions

14. mathematics test score and number of hours at volleyball practice

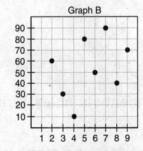

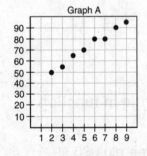

Graph A

Graph B

Graph C

Identify the correlation you would expect to see between each pair of data sets. Explain.

15. The temperature of hot coffee and the amount of time a cup of coffee sits on a desk.

16. The length of your hair and the amount of rain that fell in May.

Algebra 1

4-5 Arithmetic Sequences

Determine whether each sequence appears to be an arithmetic sequence. If so, find the common difference and the next three terms.

17. $-12.5, -10, -7.5, -5, \ldots$

18. $20, 10, -20, -10, \ldots$

19. $1\frac{1}{2}, 2\frac{1}{4}, 3, 3\frac{3}{4}, \ldots$

Find the indicated term of the arithmetic sequence.

20. $-11, -14, -17, -20, \ldots$; 13th term

21. $-6, -2, 2, 6, \ldots$; 31st term

Big Ideas

Answer these questions to summarize the important concepts from Chapter 4 in your own words.

1. Explain the difference between a continuous graph and a discrete graph. Give an example of continuous data and discrete data.

2. Explain when a relation is a function.

3. Explain the difference between an independent variable and a dependent variable.

4. Explain how to graph a function using a domain of all real numbers.

5. Write about a situation where you would expect the correlation to be negative.

6. Explain how to find the *n*th term of an arithmetic sequence.

For more review of Chapter 4:

• Complete the Chapter 4 Study Guide and Review on pages 242–245.

• Compete the Ready to Go On quizzes on pages 223 and 241.

Algebra 1

Vocabulary

This table contains important vocabulary terms from Chapter 5. As you work through the chapter, fill in the page number, definition, and a clarifying example for each term.

Term	Page	Definition	Clarifying Example
constant of variation			
direct variation			
linear function			
parallel lines			
perpendicular lines			
slope			

Algebra 1

Linear Equations and Functions

Lesson Objectives

Identify and graph linear equations and linear functions

Vocabulary

linear equation (p. 256): _____

_____

linear function (p. 256): _____

_____

Key Concepts

Standard Form of a Linear Equation (p. 258):

Standard Form of a Linear Equation
$Ax + By = C$ where A, B, and C are real numbers and A and B are not both 0:

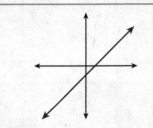 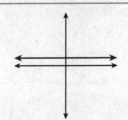 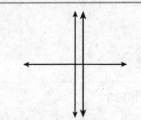

| When $A \neq 0$ and $B \neq 0$, the graph is a nonhorizontal, nonvertical line. | When $A = 0$, the graph is a horizontal line. | When $B = 0$, the graph is a vertical line. |

Algebra 1

Think and Discuss (p. 259)

Get Organized In each box, describe how to use the information to identify a linear function. Include an example.

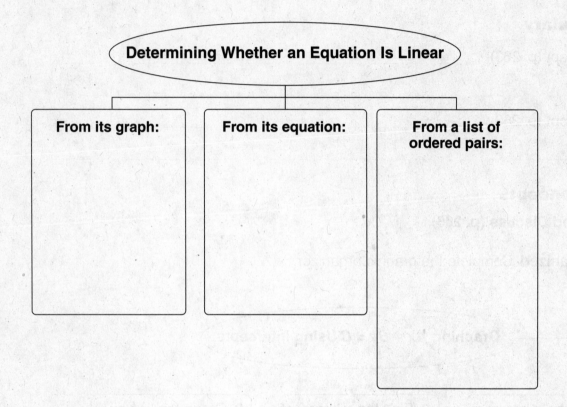

Determining Whether an Equation Is Linear

| From its graph: | From its equation: | From a list of ordered pairs: |

LESSON 5-2
Using Intercepts

Lesson Objectives

Find *x*- and *y*-intercepts and interpret their meanings in real-world situations; Use *x*- and *y*-intercepts to graph lines

Vocabulary

y-intercept (p. 263): _____

_____

x-intercept (p. 263): _____

_____

Key Concepts

Think and Discuss (p. 265)

Get Organized Complete the graphic organizer.

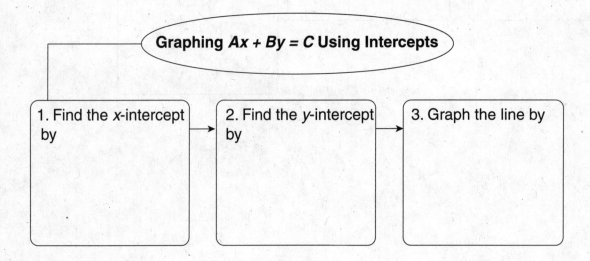

Graphing *Ax* + *By* = *C* Using Intercepts

| 1. Find the *x*-intercept by | 2. Find the *y*-intercept by | 3. Graph the line by |

Algebra 1

Slope

Lesson Objectives

Find slope of lines

Vocabulary

rate of change (p. 272) _____

_____

rise (p. 272): _____

_____

run (p. 272): _____

_____

slope (p. 272): _____

_____

Key Concepts

Slope of a Line (p. 272):

67
Algebra 1

Positive, Negative, Zero, and Undefined Slope (p. 273):

Think and Discuss (p. 276)

Get Organized In each box, show how to find slope using the given method.

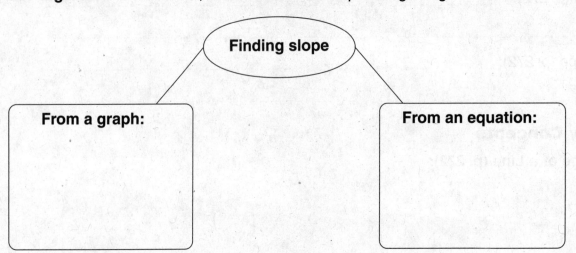

Algebra 1

Direct Variation

Lesson Objectives

Identify, write, and graph direct variation

Vocabulary

direct variation (p. 282): _____

_____

constant of variation (p. 282): _____

_____

Key Concepts

Think and Discuss (p. 285)

Get Organized In each box, describe how you can use the given information to identify a direct variation.

Recognizing a Direct Variation		
From an Equation	From Ordered Pairs	From a Graph

Algebra 1

Slope-Intercept Form

  LESSON 5-5

 Know it! Note

Lesson Objectives

Write a linear equation in slope-intercept form; Graph a line using slope-intercept form

Key Concepts

Slope-Intercept Form of a Linear Equation (p. 291):

Think and Discuss (p. 293)

Get Organized Complete the graphic organizer.

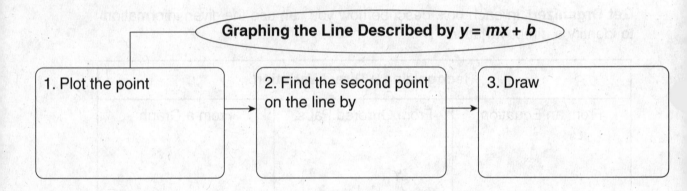

Graphing the Line Described by $y = mx + b$

1. Plot the point

2. Find the second point on the line by

3. Draw

Algebra 1

Point-Slope Form

LESSON 5-6

Know it! .Note

Lesson Objectives

Graph a line and write a linear equation using point-slope form; Write a linear equation given two points

Key Concepts

Point-Slope Form of a Linear Equation (p. 298)

Think and Discuss (p. 300)

Get Organized In each box, describe how to find the equation of a line by using each method.

Writing the Equation of a Line

If you know two points on the line:	If you know the slope and *y*-intercept:	If you know the slope and a point on the line:

Algebra 1

Slopes of Parallel and Perpendicular Lines

LESSON 5-7

Lesson Objectives

Identify and graph parallel and perpendicular lines; Write equations to describe lines parallel or perpendicular to a given line

Vocabulary

parallel lines (p. 304) _____

perpendicular lines (p. 306) _____

Key Concepts

Parallel Lines (p. 304):

Perpendicular Lines (p. 306):

Algebra 1

Think and Discuss (p. 307)

Get Organized In each box, sketch an example and describe the slopes.

Parallel lines	Perpendicular lines

Chapter Review

5-1 Linear Equations and Functions

Graph each linear equation and then tell whether it represents a function.

1. $x + 1 = 6$

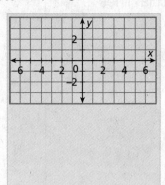

2. $-x + 4 = y$

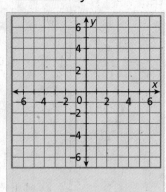

Without graphing, tell whether each point is on the graph of the given line.

3. $\frac{2}{3}x + 2 = \frac{1}{3}y$; (6, 18)

4. $-4x + 2y = 8$; (1, 6)

5-2 Using Intercepts

Use intercepts to graph the line described by each equation.

5. $2x + y = -4$

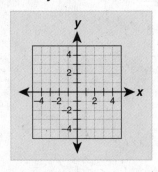

6. $3y - 12 = 1\frac{1}{2}x$

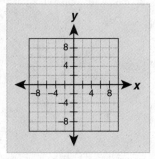

7. Brad sold tickets to a track meet. It cost $6 for an adult ticket and $3 for a student ticket. Brad sold $90 in tickets. Let x represent the number of adult tickets sold and let y represent the number of student tickets sold. Find the intercepts. What does each intercept represent?

Algebra 1

5-3 Slope

Find the slope of each line.

8.

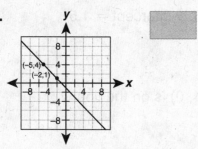

9.

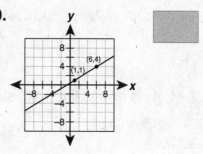

Tell whether the slope of each line is positive, negative, zero, or undefined.

10.

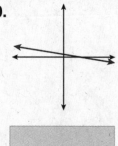

11.

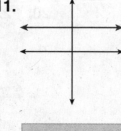

5-4 Direct Variation

Tell whether each relationship is a direct variation. If so, identify the constant of variation.

12.

x	−3	0	3	6
y	4	8	12	18

13.

x	−5	−2.5	0	2.5
y	−4	−2	0	2

14. The value of y varies directly with x, and $y = -6$ when $x = 3$. Find y when $x = 12$.

Algebra 1

5-5 Slope-Intercept Form

Write the equation of each line in slope-intercept form.

15. slope $= -3$, y-intercept $= 7$

16. slope $= 0.25$, y-intercept $= 1.5$

17. slope $= -\frac{1}{6}$, $(-4, 4)$ is on the line

18. slope $= 0$, $(4, 0)$ is on the line

Write each equation in slope-intercept form. Then graph the line given by the equation.

19. $6x = 3y + 12$

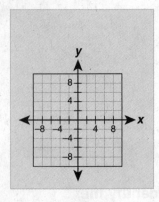

20. $-2x = 12 + 4y$

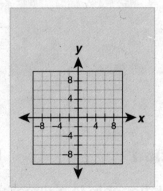

5-6 Point-Slope Form

Write an equation in slope-intercept form for the line through the two points.

21. $(-8, 2)$ and $(4, 3)$

22. $(0, 0)$ and $(6, 10)$

Algebra 1

Graph the line with the given slope that contains the given point.

23. slope = 2; (4, 2)

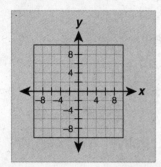

24. slope = $-\frac{1}{3}$; (1, −3)

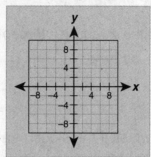

5-7 Slopes of Parallel and Perpendicular Lines

Identify which lines are parallel.

25. $y = 2(2x + 4)$; $y = 2x + 4$; $y = \frac{1}{2}(4x + 4)$; $y = 2(4x + 8)$

26. $y - \frac{1}{3} = 2x$; $y = \frac{1}{3}x + 2$; $y - \frac{1}{3} = \frac{2}{3}x + 2$; $y + \frac{1}{3} = \frac{1}{3}(6x + 2)$

27. Write an equation in slope-intercept form for the line that passes through (−3, 2) and is perpendicular to the line given by $6x - 2y = 8$.

Algebra 1

Big Ideas

Answer these questions to summarize the important concepts from Chapter 5 in your own words.

1. Explain how to find the *x*- and *y*-intercepts of a linear equation.

2. Explain how you can tell if the slope of a line is positive, negative, zero, or undefined by looking at a graph.

3. Explain the difference between slopes of parallel lines and slopes of perpendicular lines.

4. Explain why not all linear equations describe linear functions.

For more review of Chapter 5:

- Complete the Chapter 5 Study Guide and Review on pages 314–317 of your textbook.

- Complete the Ready to Go On quizzes on pages 289 and 313 of your textbook.

Algebra 1

Vocabulary

This table contains important vocabulary terms from Chapter 6. As you work through the chapter, fill in the page number, definition, and a clarifying example for each term.

Term	Page	Definition	Clarifying Example
consistent system			
dependent system			
inconsistent system			
independent system			
linear inequality			
system of linear equations			
solution of a linear inequality			
solution of a system of linear equations			
solution of a system of linear inequalities			
system of linear inequalities			

Algebra 1

Solving Systems by Graphing

LESSON 6-1

Lesson Objectives

Identify solutions of systems of linear equations in two variables; Solve systems of linear equations in two variables by graphing

Vocabulary

system of linear equations (p. 329) _____

_____

solution of a system of linear equations (p. 329) _____

_____

Key Concepts

Think and Discuss (p. 331)

Get Organized In each box, write a step for solving a linear system by graphing. More boxes may be added.

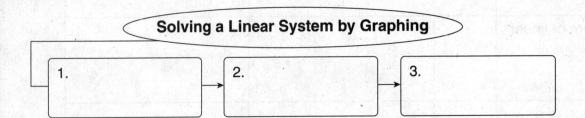

Solving a Linear System by Graphing

1.

2.

3.

Algebra 1

Solving Systems by Substitution

LESSON 6-2

Lesson Objectives

Solve systems of linear equations in two variables by substitution

Key Concepts

Solving Systems of Equations by Using Substitution (p. 336):

Solving Systems of Equations by Substitution	
Step 1	
Step 2	
Step 3	
Step 4	
Step 5	

Think and Discuss (p. 339)

Get Organized In each box, solve the system by substitution using the first step given. Show that each method gives the same solution.

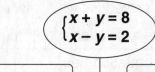

$$\begin{cases} x + y = 8 \\ x - y = 2 \end{cases}$$

Solve $x + y = 8$ for x.	Solve $x + y = 8$ for y.

Solve $x - y = 2$ for x.	Solve $x - y = 2$ for y.

Algebra 1

LESSON 6-3

Solving Systems by Elimination

Lesson Objectives

Solve systems of linear equations in two variables by elimination; Compare and choose an appropriate method for solving systems of linear equations

Key Concepts

Solving Systems of Equations by Using Elimination (p. 343):

Solving Systems of Equations by Elimination
Step 1
Step 2
Step 3
Step 4
Step 5

Systems of Linear Equations (p. 346):

METHOD	USE WHEN . . .	EXAMPLE
Graphing	• Both equations are solved for y. • You want to estimate a solution.	$\begin{cases} y = 3x + 2 \\ y = -2x + 6 \end{cases}$
Substitution	• A variable in either equation has a coefficient of 1 or -1. • Both equations are solved for the same variable. • Either equation is solved for a variable.	$\begin{cases} x + 2y = 7 \\ x = 10 - 5y \end{cases}$ or $\begin{cases} x = 2y + 10 \\ x = 3y + 5 \end{cases}$
Elimination	• Both equations have the same variable with the same or opposite coefficients. • A variable term in one equation is a multiple of the corresponding variable term in the other equation.	$\begin{cases} 3x + 2y = 8 \\ 5x + 2y = 12 \end{cases}$ or $\begin{cases} 6x + 5y = 10 \\ 3x + 2y = 15 \end{cases}$

Algebra 1

Think and Discuss (p. 347)

Get Organized In each box, write an example of a system of equations that you could solve using the given method.

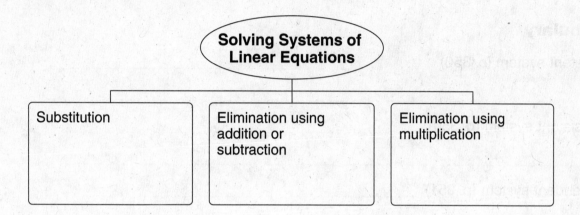

Solving Special Systems

LESSON 6-4

Lesson Objectives

Solve special systems of linear equations in two variables; Classify systems of linear equations and determine the number of solutions

Vocabulary

consistent system (p. 350) _____

_____

inconsistent system (p. 350) _____

_____

independent system (p. 351) _____

_____

dependent system (p. 351) _____

Algebra 1

Key Concepts

Classification of Systems of Linear Equations (p. 351):

CLASSIFICATION	CONSISTENT AND INDEPENDENT	CONSISTENT AND DEPENDENT	INCONSISTENT
Number of Solutions			
Description			
Graph			

Think and Discuss (p. 353)

Get Organized In each box, write the word that describes a system with that number of solutions and sketch a graph.

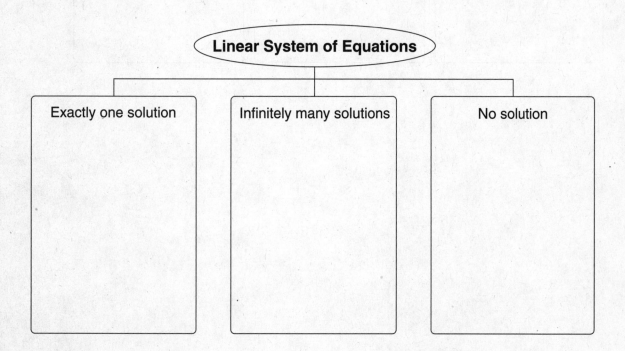

Linear System of Equations
Exactly one solution	Infinitely many solutions	No solution

Algebra 1

LESSON 6-5

Applying Systems

Lesson Objectives

Use systems of equations to solve application problems

Key Concepts

Think and Discuss (p. 359)

Get Organized In each box, write an example of each type of problem and find the solution.

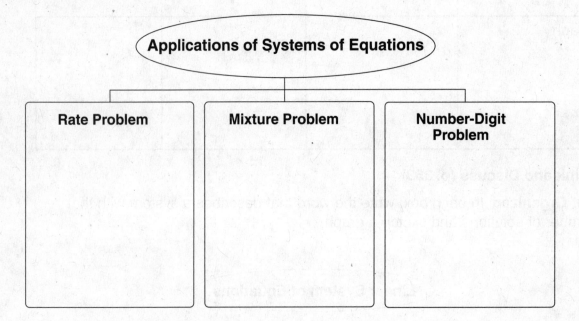

Applications of Systems of Equations

Rate Problem	Mixture Problem	Number-Digit Problem

Algebra 1

LESSON 6-6
Solving Linear Inequalities

Lesson Objectives

Graph and solve linear inequalities in two variables

Vocabulary

linear inequality (p. 364) _____

_____

solution of a linear inequality (p. 364) _____

_____

Key Concepts

Graphing Inequalities (p. 365):

Graphing Linear Inequalities	
Step 1	
Step 2	
Step 3	

Think and Discuss (p. 367)

Get Organized Complete the graphic organizer.

Inequality	$y < 5x + 2$	$y > 7x - 3$	$y \leq 9x + 1$	$y \geq -3x - 2$
Symbol	$<$			
Boundary Line	Dashed			
Shading	Below			

Algebra 1

LESSON 6-7 **Solving Systems of Linear Inequalities**

Lesson Objectives

Graph and solve systems of linear inequalities in two variables

Vocabulary

system of linear inequalities (p. 371) _____

_____

solution of a system of linear inequalities (p. 371) _____

_____

Key Concepts

Think and Discuss (p. 373)

Get Organized In each box, draw a graph and list one solution.

$$\begin{cases} y \geq 2x + 1 \\ y > \frac{1}{2}x - 2 \end{cases}$$

$$\begin{cases} y < 2x + 1 \\ y \geq \frac{1}{2}x - 2 \end{cases}$$

Graph	Solution	Graph	Solution

Algebra 1

6-1 Solving Systems by Graphing

Tell whether the ordered pair is a solution of the given system.

1. $(2, -3)$; $\begin{cases} 2x - y = 7 \\ x - 2y = -5 \end{cases}$ **2.** $(-1, -5)$; $\begin{cases} y = 3x - 2 \\ y = -x - 6 \end{cases}$ **3.** $(3, 14)$; $\begin{cases} x = \frac{1}{2}y - 4 \\ y = 4x + 2 \end{cases}$

Solve each system by graphing.

4. $\begin{cases} x - 2y = 3 \\ y + x = 0 \end{cases}$

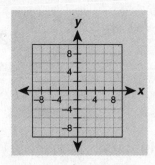

5. $\begin{cases} x = 6 - y \\ 2 - x = -y \end{cases}$

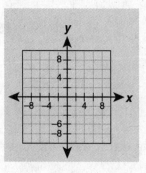

6-2 Solving Systems by Substitution

Solve each system by substitution.

6. $\begin{cases} x + 2y = 16 \\ x - 3y = 1 \end{cases}$ **7.** $\begin{cases} 7x + 5y = 175 \\ x + y = 23 \end{cases}$ **8.** $\begin{cases} 2x + y = -9 \\ 3x + 4y = -11 \end{cases}$

9. The sum of two numbers is 66. The second number is 22 less than three times the first number. Write and solve a system of equations to find the two numbers.

6-3 Solving Systems by Elimination

Solve each system by elimination.

10. $\begin{cases} 4y = 25 - 3x \\ 4x = 7y - 16 \end{cases}$ **11.** $\begin{cases} 3x - y = -137 \\ y = 2x + 99 \end{cases}$ **12.** $\begin{cases} 2x + y = -21 \\ 12x - 13y = 387 \end{cases}$

Algebra 1

13. John needs 23 boards to build rafters for his house. He can use 16-foot or 20-foot length boards. He needs seven fewer 16-foot boards than 20-foot boards. Write and solve a system of equations to determine how many of each size board John needs.

6-4 Solving Special Systems

Solve each system of linear equations.

14. $\begin{cases} 4y - 6x = 10 \\ 15 + 9x = 6y \end{cases}$

15. $\begin{cases} 2x - 5y = 15 \\ 10y = 20 + 4x \end{cases}$

16. $\begin{cases} 6x + 14y = 16 \\ 24 - 9x = 21y \end{cases}$

Classify each system. Give the number of solutions.

17. $\begin{cases} y - 3x = 3 \\ 3(x - 1) = y \end{cases}$

18. $\begin{cases} y + x = 3 \\ 6 = 2x - y \end{cases}$

19. $\begin{cases} 3x = -y - 2 \\ 2y + 4 = -6x \end{cases}$

6-5 Applying Systems

20. Alice wants to make one pound of a dried fruit mix of strawberries and bananas. She has $1.75 to spend. Dried strawberries cost $2.75 per pound and dried bananas cost $1.25 per pound. Write and solve a system of equations to find the amount of dried strawberries and dried bananas Alice should purchase.

Algebra 1

21. With a tailwind a plane makes a 1500-mile trip in 2.5 hours. On the return trip, the plane flies against the same wind and covers 1500 miles in 3 hours. Solve to find the speed of the wind and the speed of the plane.

6-6 Solving Linear Inequalities

Tell whether the ordered pair is a solution of the inequality.

22. $(-4, 2)$; $y \geq 2x - 4$ **23.** $(6, 8)$; $y < 2x - 4$ **24.** $(1, 2)$; $2y \leq x + 3$

Graph the solutions of each linear inequality.

25. $y \geq 2x - 2$

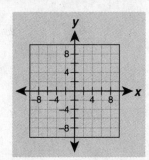

26. $y + \frac{1}{2}x \leq 1$

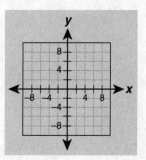

6-7 Solving Systems of Linear Inequalities

Tell whether the ordered pair is a solution of the given system.

27. $(0, 0)$; $\begin{cases} x + 2y < 4 \\ 2y > x - 6 \end{cases}$ **28.** $(-2, 2)$; $\begin{cases} y \geq x + 3 \\ 2x \geq 3y + 2 \end{cases}$ **29.** $(4, -3)$; $\begin{cases} 2y - x < -6 \\ 2x \geq -3y \end{cases}$

Graph each system of linear inequalities.

30. $\begin{cases} 2x - y > -3 \\ 4x + y < 5 \end{cases}$

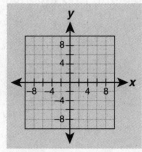

31. $\begin{cases} x - y < -2 \\ x - y > 2 \end{cases}$

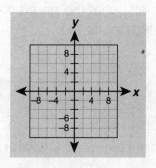

Algebra 1

Answer these questions to summarize the important concepts from Chapter 6 in your own words.

1. What are the steps for solving systems of equations by using substitution?

2. Explain which method is best for solving systems of linear equations for certain systems.

3. What are the steps for graphing inequalities?

4. Explain what the graph of a dependent, consistent, and inconsistent system looks like.

For more review of Chapter 6:

- Complete the Chapter 6 Study Guide and Review on pages 430–433.

- Compete the Ready to Go On quizzes on pages 413 and 429.

Algebra 1

Vocabulary

This table contains important vocabulary terms from Chapter 7. As you work through the chapter, fill in the page number, definition, and a clarifying example for each term.

Term	Page	Definition	Clarifying Example
binomial			
degree of a monomial			
degree of a polynomial			
index			
leading coefficient			
monomial			
perfect-square trinomial			
polynomial			
scientific notation			
trinomial			

Algebra 1

Integer Exponents

Lesson Objectives

Evaluate expressions containing integer exponents; Simplify
expressions containing integer exponents

Key Concepts

Integer Exponents (p. 394):

WORDS	NUMBERS	ALGEBRA

Think and Discuss (p. 396)

Get Organized In each box, describe how to simplify, and give an example.

```
        ┌─────────────────────────────┐
        │  Simplifying Expressions with │
        │     Negative Exponents        │
        └─────────────────────────────┘
```

For a negative exponent in the numerator . . .	For a negative exponent in the denominator . . .

Algebra 1

Powers of 10 and Scientific Notation

Lesson Objectives

Evaluate and multiply by powers of 10; Convert between standard notation and scientific notation

Vocabulary

scientific notation (p. 401) _____

_____

Key Concepts

Powers of 10 (p. 400):

WORDS	NUMBERS
Positive Integer Exponent	
Negative Integer Exponent	

Multiplying by Powers of 10 (p. 401):

Algebra 1

Think and Discuss (p. 402)

Get Organized Complete the graphic organizer.

```
            ( Powers of 10 and Scientific Notation )
                  ┌──────────────┴──────────────┐
  ┌───────────────────────────────┐   ┌───────────────────────────────┐
  │ A negative exponent corresponds to │   │ A positive exponent corresponds to │
  │ moving the decimal point        .  │   │ moving the decimal point        .  │
  └───────────────────────────────┘   └───────────────────────────────┘
```

Algebra 1

Multiplication Properties of Exponents

LESSON 7-3

Lesson Objectives

Use multiplication properties of exponents to evaluate and simplify expressions

Key Concepts

Simplifying Exponential Expressions (p. 408):

Simplifying Exponential Expressions
An exponential expression is completely simplified if . . .

Examples	Nonexamples

Product of Powers Property (p. 408):

WORDS	NUMBERS	ALGEBRA

Power of a Power Property (p. 410):

WORDS	NUMBERS	ALGEBRA

Algebra 1

Power of a Product Property (p. 411):

WORDS	NUMBERS	ALGEBRA

Think and Discuss (p. 411)

Get Organized In each box give an example for each property.

Multiplication Properties of Exponents		
Product of Powers Property	Power of a Power Property	Power of a Product Property

Algebra 1

Division Properties of Exponents

Lesson Objectives

Use division properties of exponents to evaluate and simplify expressions

Key Concepts

Quotient of Powers Property (p. 415):

WORDS	NUMBERS	ALGEBRA

Positive Power of a Quotient Property (p. 417):

WORDS	NUMBERS	ALGEBRA

Negative Power of a Quotient Property (p. 418):

WORDS	NUMBERS	ALGEBRA

Algebra 1

Think and Discuss (p. 419)

Get Organized In each box, supply the missing information. Then give an example for each property.

If a and b are nonzero real numbers and m and n are integers, then...		
$\dfrac{a^m}{a^n} =$	$\left(\dfrac{a}{b}\right)^n =$	$\left(\dfrac{a}{b}\right)^{-n} =$

Fractional Exponents

Lesson Objectives

Evaluate and simplify expressions containing fractional exponents.

Vocabulary

index (p. 422) _____

_____

Key Concepts

Definition of $b^{\frac{1}{n}}$ (p. 422)

WORDS	NUMBERS	ALGEBRA

Definition of $b^{\frac{m}{n}}$ (p. 423)

WORDS	NUMBERS	ALGEBRA

Algebra 1

Think and Discuss (p. 424)

Get Organized In each box, provide the definition and a numerical example of each type of fractional exponent.

Fractional Exponent	Definition	Numerical Example
$b^{\frac{1}{n}}$		
$b^{\frac{m}{n}}$		

Algebra 1

Lesson Objectives

Classify polynomials and write polynomials in standard form; Evaluate polynomial expressions

Vocabulary

monomial (p. 430) _____

_____

degree of a monomial (p. 430) _____

_____

polynomial (p. 430) _____

_____

degree of a polynomial (p. 430) _____

_____

standard form of a polynomial (p. 430) _____

_____

leading coefficient (p. 430) _____

_____

quadratic (p. 431) _____

_____

cubic (p. 431) _____

_____

binomial (p. 431) _____

_____

trinomial (p. 431) _____

_____

root (p. 432) _____

_____

Key Concepts

Think and Discuss (p. 432)

Get Organized In each circle, write an example of the given type of polynomial.

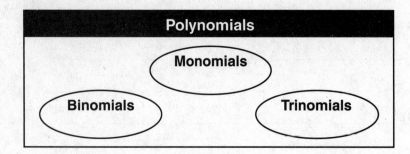

Algebra 1

Adding and Subtracting Polynomials

Lesson Objectives

Add and subtract polynomials

Key Concepts

Think and Discuss (p. 440)

Get Organized In each box, write an example that shows how to perform the given operation.

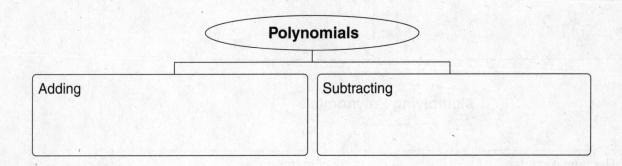

Algebra 1

Multiplying Polynomials

LESSON 7-8

Lesson Objectives

Multiply polynomials

Key Concepts

Think and Discuss (p. 450)

Get Organized In each box, multiply two polynomials using the given method.

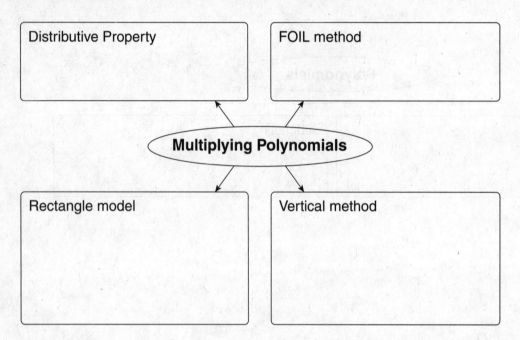

| Distributive Property | FOIL method |

Multiplying Polynomials

| Rectangle model | Vertical method |

Algebra 1

Special Products of Binomials

Lesson Objectives

Find special products of binomials

Vocabulary

perfect-square trinomial (p. 455): _____

_____

difference of two squares (p. 457): _____

_____

Key Concepts

Special Products of Binomials (p. 458):

Special Products of Binomials

Think and Discuss (p. 459)

Get Organized Complete the special product rules and give an example of each.

Special Products of Binomials		
Perfect-Square Trinomials		Difference of Two Squares
$(a + b)^2 =$	$(a - b)^2 =$	$(a + b)(a - b) =$

Algebra 1

Chapter Review

7-1 Integer Exponents

Simplify.

1. $25g^0$

2. $s^{-2}r^3$

3. $\dfrac{3p^{-2}g^{-3}}{2t^0}$

4. $\dfrac{1}{3}x^{-2}y^4$

Evaluate each expression for the given value(s) of the variable(s).

5. $(b - 4)^{-3}$ for $b = 4$ **6.** x^2y^0 for $x = 3$ and $y = 6$ **7.** $(2mn)^{-2} m = 3$ and $n = -2$

7-2 Powers of 10 and Scientific Notation

8. Find the value of 10^{-6}.

9. Write 10,000,000 as a power of 10.

10. Find the value of 14.2×10^3

11. Write 0.0000001715 in scientific notation.

12. The average diameter of a human hair is 0.00006 meters. Write this number in scientific notation.

Algebra 1

7-3 Multiplication Properties of Exponents

Simplify.

13. $4^4 \cdot 4^{-5} \cdot 4^3$ **14.** $x^{-2} \cdot x^3 \cdot y^5$ **15.** $(-2s^2t^3)^2$ **16.** $(m^2n)^4 \cdot (m^4n^3)^2$

17. $(2xy^2)^4 \cdot (x^2y)^{-3}$ **18.** $-(r^2)^{-3} \cdot (-r^2)^3$ **19.** $(x^by^{2r})^3$ **20.** $(x+2)^{-3} \cdot (x+2)$

7-4 Division Properties of Exponents

Simplify.

21. $\dfrac{x^6}{x^3}$ **22.** $\left(\dfrac{4}{5}\right)^3$ **23.** $\dfrac{x^4y^3}{x^2y^4}$ **24.** $\left(\dfrac{rs^4}{r^4s^2}\right)^{-2}$

25. In 1867, the United States purchased Alaska from Russia for $7.2 million. The total area of Alaska is about 3.78×10^8 acres. What was the price per acre? Write your answer in standard form.

7-5 Fractional Exponents

Fill in the boxes to make each statement true.

26. $4^{\frac{\boxed{}}{2}} = 8$ **27.** $81^{\frac{3}{\boxed{}}} = 27$

Simplify each expression.

28. $25^{\frac{1}{2}}$ **29.** $49^{\frac{1}{2}} + 8^{\frac{1}{3}}$ **30.** $256^{\frac{3}{4}}$ **31.** $1^{\frac{7}{2}}$

Algebra 1

7-6 Polynomials

Write each polynomial in standard form and give the leading coefficient.

32. $-4x^2 - x^3 + 3$

33. $15y - 6 + 10y^3 - 3y^2$

Classify each polynomial according to its degree and number of terms.

34. $6x + 3x^2 + 1$

35. $16 - 4x^3 + 3x^2$

7-7 Adding and Subtracting Polynomials

Add or subtract.

36. $(-3y + 2) + (y^2 + 3y + 2)$

37. $(2x^2 + 3x - 4) - (x^2 + x - 1)$

38. $(-2x^3 - x + 8) - (-2x^3 + 3x - 4)$

39. $(-4x^3 - 2x^2 + x - 5) + (2x^3 + 3x + 4)$

7-8 Multiplying Polynomials

Multiply.

40. $(3x - 7)(-2x)$

41. $3x^2(5x - x^3 + 2)$

42. $(3x - 2)(5x + 7)$

43. $(x - 5)(2x + 10)$

44. $(x^2 + 9)(x^2 - x - 4)$

45. $(2x^2 - 7x + 1)(4x + 3)$

Algebra 1

7-9 Special Products of Binomials

Multiply.

46. $(2x + 1)^2$

47. $(2 + 3y)^2$

48. $(3y - 2)^2$

49. $(4x + 3y)^2$

50. $(5x - 6)(5x + 6)$

51. $(4x - 7y)(4x + 7y)$

52. The height traveled (in feet) of a bottle rocket is modeled by $h = -16t^2 + 57t$ where *t* is the time in seconds. Find the height of the rocket after 2 seconds.

Algebra 1

Big Ideas

Answer these questions to summarize the important concepts from Chapter 7 in your own words.

1. Explain why the properties using zero exponents and negative exponents specify that bases must be "nonzero numbers".

2. Explain the difference between multiplying by powers of 10 when the exponent is a positive number and when the exponent is a negative number.

3. When is an exponential expression completely simplified?

4. Explain how to multiply $(x + 3)(x + 2)$ using the FOIL method.

For more review of Chapter 7:

- Complete the Chapter 7 Study Guide and Review on pages 464–467.
- Compete the Ready to Go On quizzes on pages 429 and 463.

Algebra 1

Vocabulary

This table contains important vocabulary terms from Chapter 8. As you work through the chapter, fill in the page number, definition, and a clarifying example for each term.

Term	Page	Definition	Clarifying Example
contradiction			
greatest common factor			
indirect proof			
prime factorization			

Algebra 1

LESSON 8-1
Factors and Greatest Common Factors

Lesson Objectives

Write the prime factorization of numbers; Find the GCF of monomials

Vocabulary

prime factorization (p. 478): _____

_____

greatest common factor (p. 479): _____

_____

Key Concepts

Think and Discuss (p. 480)

Get Organized Show how to write the prime factorization of $100x^2$ by filling in each box.

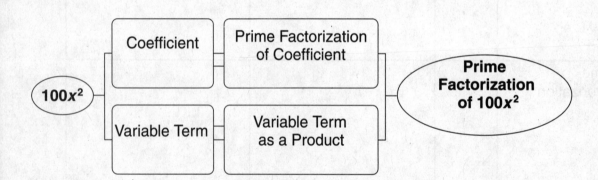

Algebra 1

Factoring by GCF

Know it!
.Note

Lesson Objectives

Factor polynomials by using the greatest common factor

Key Concepts

Think and Discuss (p. 490)

Get Organized Complete the graphic organizer.

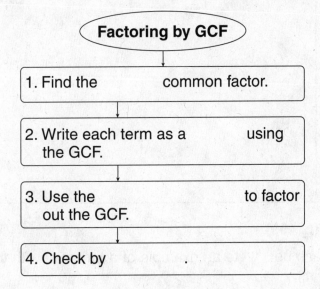

Factoring by GCF

1. Find the _____ common factor.

2. Write each term as a _____ using the GCF.

3. Use the _____ to factor out the GCF.

4. Check by _____.

Algebra 1

LESSON 8-3 Factoring $x^2 + bx + c$

Lesson Objectives

Factor quadratic trinomials of the form $x^2 + bx + c$

Key Concepts

Factoring $x^2 + bx + c$ (p. 497):

WORDS	EXAMPLE

Think and Discuss (p. 499)

Get Organized In each box, write an example of a trinomial with the given properties and factor it.

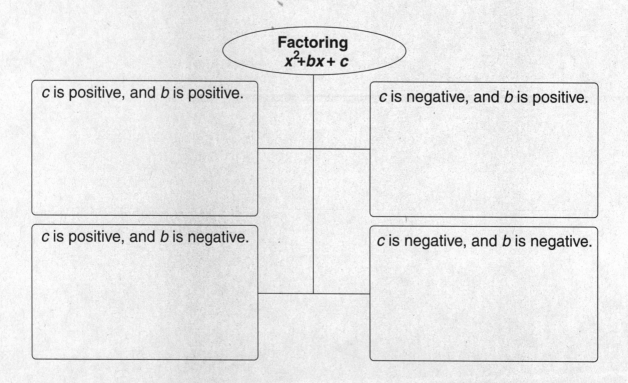

Factoring
$x^2 + bx + c$

c is positive, and b is positive.

c is negative, and b is positive.

c is positive, and b is negative.

c is negative, and b is negative.

Algebra 1

Factoring $ax^2 + bx + c$

Lesson Objectives

Factor quadratic trinomials of the form $ax^2 + bx + c$

Key Concepts

Think and Discuss (p. 508)

Get Organized Write each of the following trinomials in the appropriate box and factor each one.

$3x^2 + 10x - 8$

$3x^2 - 10x + 8$

$3x^2 + 10x + 8$

$3x^2 - 10x - 8$

Factoring $ax^2 + bx + c$	
$c > 0$	
$b > 0$	$b < 0$
$c < 0$	
$b < 0$	$b > 0$

Algebra 1

LESSON 8-5
Factoring Special Products

Lesson Objectives

Factor perfect-square trinomials; Factor the difference of two squares

Key Concepts

Factoring Perfect-Square Trinomials (p. 514):

PERFECT-SQUARE TRINOMIAL	EXAMPLES

Factoring a Difference of Two Squares (p. 516):

DIFFERENCE OF TWO SQUARES	EXAMPLE

Think and Discuss (p. 517)

Get Organized Write an example of each type of special product and factor it.

Special Product	Factored Form
Perfect-square trinomial with positive coefficient of middle term	
Perfect-square trinomial with negative coefficient of middle term	
Difference of two squares	

Algebra 1

Choosing a Factoring Method

Lesson Objectives

Choose an appropriate method for factoring a polynomial; Combine methods for factoring a polynomial

Key Concepts

Methods to Factor Polynomials (p. 524):

METHODS TO FACTOR POLYNOMIALS	
Any Polynomial	
Binomials	
Trinomials	
Polynomials of Four or More Terms	

Think and Discuss (p. 524)

Get Organized Draw an arrow from each expression to the method you would use to factor it.

Factoring Methods		
Polynomial		**Method**
1. $16x^4 - 25y^8$	**A.**	Factoring out the GCF
2. $x^2 + 10x + 25$	**B.**	Factoring by grouping
3. $9t^2 + 27t + 18t^4$	**C.**	Unfactorable
4. $a^2 + 3a - 7a - 21$	**D.**	Difference of two squares
5. $100b^2 + 81$	**E.**	Perfect-square trinomial

Algebra 1

8-1 Factors and Greatest Common Factors

Write the prime factorization of each number.

1. 66

2. 72

3. 325

4. 169

Find the GCF of each pair of monomials.

5. $30r^4$ and $12r^3$

6. $24z^3$ and $32z^2$

7. $16x^2y$ and $84xy^2$

8. $99s^6t^3$ and $45s^3t^6$

8-2 Factoring by GCF

Factor each polynomial. Check your answer.

9. $2s^2 - 4$

10. $-a^3 - 4a$

11. $36y^4 + 24y^2$

12. $4x^2 - 8x + 8$

13. $3b^3 - 15b^2 - 33b$

14. $14p^3 - 21p^2q$

Factor each polynomial by grouping. Check your answer.

15. $r^3 + 3r^2 + 2r + 6$

16. $7y^3 - 14y^2 - y + 2$

17. $5x^3 + 10x^2 + 3x + 6$

Algebra 1

8-3 Factoring $x^2 + bx + c$

Factor each trinomial. Check your answer.

18. $a^2 - 5a - 14$

19. $x^2 + 7x + 10$

20. $n^2 + 4n - 12$

21. $f^2 - 11f + 18$

22. $z^2 - z - 20$

23. $t^2 - t - 30$

24. Factor $x^2 - 7x + 12$. Check your answer.

8-4 Factoring $ax^2 + bx + c$

Factor each trinomial. Check your answer.

25. $3a^2 + 5a + 2$

26. $6s^2 + 17s + 12$

27. $5y^2 - 18y - 8$

28. $10z^2 + 12z - 16$

29. $21x^2 + 44x - 32$

30. $6t^2 - 31t + 35$

31. The area of a rectangle is $5x^2 + 22x + 8$ cm^2. The width is $(x + 4)$ cm.

What is the length of the rectangle?

8-5 Factoring Special Products

Determine whether each trinomial is a perfect square. If so, factor.

32. $9t^2 - 30t + 25$

33. $z^2 + 8z - 16$

34. $4y^2 + 36y + 81$

35. $4x^2 - 28x + 49$

36. $b^2 - 16b + 64$

37. $16m^2 + 12m + 9$

Determine whether each trinomial is the difference of two squares. If so, factor.

38. $1 - 10s^4$

39. $t^2 - 9$

40. $121x^2 - 100$

41. $25h^2 - 20$

42. $9z^4 + 25$

43. $25y^4 - 16x^2$

8-6 Choosing a Factoring Method

Factor each polynomial completely. Check your answer.

44. $25b^3 + 30b^2 - 60b$

45. $2x^2y + 16xy + 30y$

46. $c^3 - 6c^2 - 4c + 24$

Write an expression for the situation. Factor your expression.

47. Nine times the square of Teresa's shoe size plus twelve times Teresa's shoe size plus four

48. The difference of the square of four times a DVD cost and 49

Algebra 1

Big Ideas

Answer these questions to summarize the important concepts from Chapter 8 in your own words.

1. Explain how to find the GCF of two terms that contain the same variable raised to different exponents.

2. What are the steps for factoring the GCF?

3. Explain, in words, how to factor the quadratic trinomial $x^2 + bx + c$.

4. Explain how to determine the signs of the factors of c when factoring a trinomial of the form $x^2 + bx + c$.

For more review of Chapter 8:

- Complete the Chapter 8 Study Guide and Review on pages 530–533 of your textbook.

- Compete the Ready to Go On quizzes on pages 513 and 529 of your textbook.

Algebra 1

Vocabulary

This table contains important vocabulary terms from Chapter 9. As you work through the chapter, fill in the page number, definition, and a clarifying example for each term.

Term	Page	Definition	Clarifying Example
axis of symmetry			
completing the square			
discriminant			
quadratic equation			
vertex			

Algebra 1

Quadratic Equations and Functions

Lesson Objectives

Identify quadratic functions and determine whether they have a minimum or maximum; Graph a quadratic function and give its domain and range

Vocabulary

quadratic equation (p. 544): _____

_____

quadratic function (p. 544): _____

_____

parabola (p. 545): _____

_____

vertex (p. 546): _____

_____

minimum value (p. 546): _____

_____

maximum value (p. 546): _____

_____

Algebra 1

Key Concepts

Minimum and Maximum Values of Quadratic Functions (p. 546):

WORDS		
GRAPHS		

Think and Discuss (p. 547)

Get Organized In each box, sketch and describe the graph and tell whether the function has a maximum value or a minimum value.

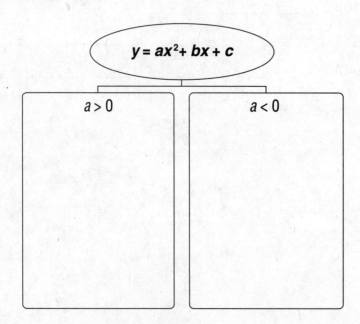

Algebra 1

Characteristics of Quadratic Functions

LESSON 9-2

Lesson Objectives

Find the zeros of a quadratic function from its graph; Find the axis of symmetry and the vertex of a parabola

Vocabulary

zero of a function (p. 553): _____

_____

axis of symmetry (p. 554): _____

_____

Key Concepts

Finding the Axis of Symmetry by Using Zeros (p. 554):

WORDS	NUMBERS	GRAPH
One Zero		
Two Zeros		

Finding the Axis of Symmetry by Using the Formula (p. 555):

FORMULA	EXAMPLE

Finding the Vertex of a Parabola (p. 555):

FINDING THE VERTEX OF A PARABOLA
Step 1
Step 2
Step 3

Think and Discuss (p. 557)

Get Organized In each box, sketch a graph that fits the given description.

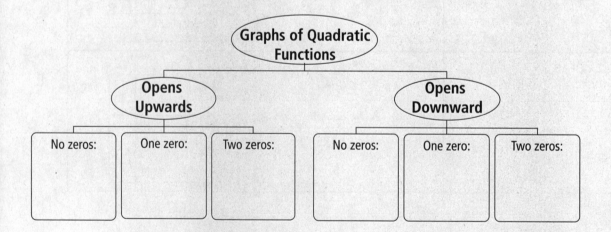

Algebra 1

Graphing Quadratic Functions

Lesson Objectives

Graph a quadratic function in the form $y = ax^2 + bx + c$

Key Concepts

Think and Discuss (p. 563)

Get Organized Complete the graphic organizer using your own quadratic function.

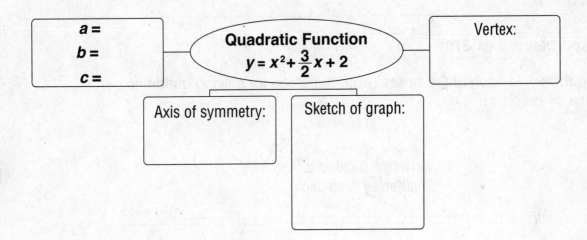

a =

b =

c =

Quadratic Function

$y = x^2 + \dfrac{3}{2}x + 2$

Vertex:

Axis of symmetry:

Sketch of graph:

Algebra 1

Solving Quadratic Equations by Graphing

LESSON 9-4

Know it!
.Note

Lesson Objectives

Solve quadratic equations by graphing

Key Concepts

Solving Quadratic Equations by Graphing (p. 568):

Step 1	
Step 2	
Step 3	

Think and Discuss (p. 570)

Get Organized In each of the boxes, write the steps for solving quadratic equations by graphing.

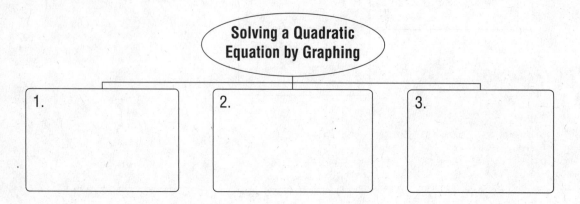

Solving a Quadratic Equation by Graphing

1.

2.

3.

Algebra 1

Solving Quadratic Equations by Factoring

LESSON 9-5

 Know it! Note

Lesson Objectives

Solve quadratic equations by factoring

Key Concepts

Zero Product Property (p. 576):

For all real numbers a and b,		
WORDS	**NUMBERS**	**ALGEBRA**

Think and Discuss (p. 579)

Get Organized In each box, write a step used to solve a quadratic equation by factoring.

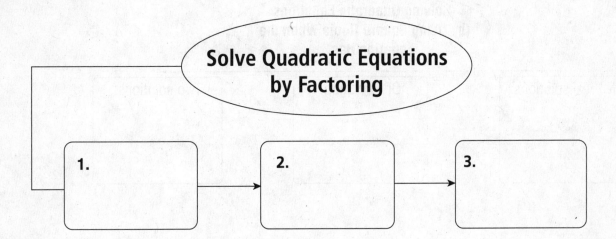

Solve Quadratic Equations by Factoring

1.

2.

3.

131

Algebra 1

LESSON 9-6 Solving Quadratic Equations by Using Square Roots

Lesson Objectives

Solve quadratic equations by using square roots

Key Concepts

Square-Root Property (p. 582):

WORDS	NUMBERS	ALGEBRA

Think and Discuss (p. 585)

Get Organized In each box, write an example of a quadratic equation with the given number of solutions. Solve each equation.

Solving Quadratic Equations by Using Square Roots When the Equation Has....

No real solutions:	One solution:	Two solutions:

132

Algebra 1

Completing the Square

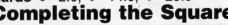

LESSON 9-7

Lesson Objectives

Solve quadratic equations by completing the square

Vocabulary

completing the square (p. 591): _____

_____

Key Concepts

Completing the Square (p. 591):

WORDS	NUMBERS	ALGEBRA

Solving a Quadratic Equation by Completing the Square (p. 592):

Step 1
Step 2
Step 3
Step 4
Step 5
Step 6

Algebra 1

Think and Discuss (p. 594)

Get Organized In each box, write and solve an example using the given type of quadratic equation.

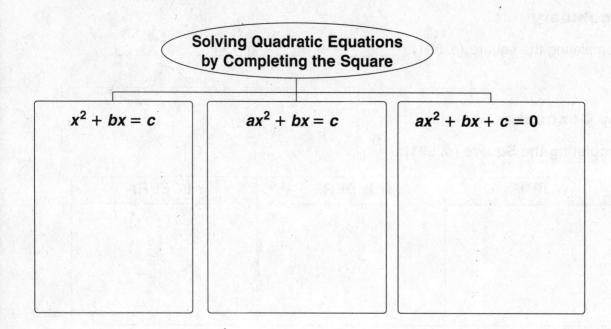

Solving Quadratic Equations by Completing the Square

| $x^2 + bx = c$ | $ax^2 + bx = c$ | $ax^2 + bx + c = 0$ |

LESSON 9-8 The Quadratic Formula

Lesson Objectives

Solve quadratic equations by using the Quadratic Formula

Key Concepts

The Quadratic Formula (p. 598):

| |
| |

Methods of Solving Quadratic Equations (p. 601):

METHOD	ADVANTAGES	DISADVANTAGES
Graphing		
Factoring		
Using square roots		
Completing the square		
Using the Quadratic Formula		

Algebra 1

Think and Discuss (p. 601)

Get Organized In each box, write the method you would use to solve each equation and explain why.

Equation	$x^2 + 5 = 20$	$x^2 + 6x + 9 = 0$	$3x^2 - 7x + 11 = 0$
Method			

Algebra 1

LESSON 9-9

The Discriminant

Lesson Objectives

Determine the number of solutions of a quadratic equation by using the discriminant

Vocabulary

discriminant (p. 605): _____

_____

Key Concepts

The Discriminant of the Quadratic Equation $ax^2 + bx + c = 0$ (p. 605):

Think and Discuss (p. 607)

Get Organized In each box, write the number of real solutions.

$$\text{The number of real solutions of } ax + bx + c = 0 \text{ when . . .}$$

| $b^2 - 4ac > 0$ | $b^2 - 4ac < 0$ | $b^2 - 4ac = 0$ |

Algebra 1

Chapter Review

9-1 Quadratic Equations and Functions

Without graphing, tell whether each point is on the graph of $y = -2x^2 + 6$.

1. $(2, 3)$

2. $(2, -2)$

Tell whether the graph of each quadratic function opens upward or downward and whether the parabola has a maximum or a minimum.

3. $y = -x^2 + 4x - 1$

4. $y = 2x^2 + 3x + 5$

5. Graph the function $y = -\frac{3}{4}x^2 - x + 4$ and give the domain and range.

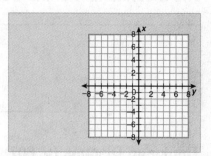

9-2 Characteristics of Quadratic Functions

Find the zeros of each function from its graph. Then find its axis of symmetry.

6.
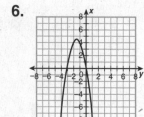

7.
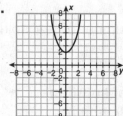

8.
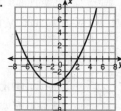

Find the vertex of each parabola.

9. $y = x^2 + 6x - 7$

10. $y = x^2 - 10x + 21$

11. $y = 3x^2 + 9x - 12$

Algebra 1

9-3 Graphing Quadratic Functions

Graph each quadratic function.

12. $y = 2x^2 + 6x + 1$ **13.** $y + 3x^2 = \frac{1}{3}x - 1$ **14.** $y = \frac{1}{4}x^2 - 2x + 4$

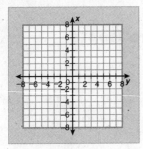 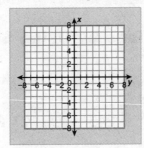 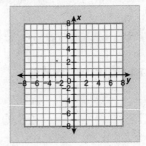

9-4 Solving Quadratic Equations by Graphing

Solve each equation by graphing the related function.

15. $x^2 - 4x = 0$ **16.** $2x - 3 = -\frac{1}{3}x^2$ **17.** $-8x^2 - 4 = -16x$

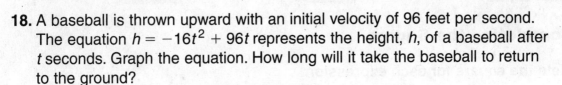

18. A baseball is thrown upward with an initial velocity of 96 feet per second. The equation $h = -16t^2 + 96t$ represents the height, h, of a baseball after t seconds. Graph the equation. How long will it take the baseball to return to the ground?

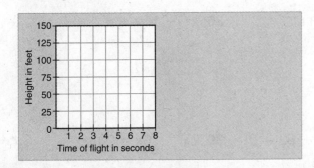

9-5 Solving Quadratic Equations by Factoring

Use the Zero Product Property to solve each equation.

19. $(x - 5)(x + 2) = 0$ **20.** $(2x - 5)(4x - 5) = 0$ **21.** $x(x - 5) = 0$

Algebra 1

Solve each quadratic equation by factoring.

22. $x^2 + 5x + 6 = 0$ **23.** $2x^2 + 5x = 12$ **24.** $4x^2 = 4x - 1$

9-6 Solving Quadratic Equations by Using Square Roots

Solve using square roots.

25. $2x^2 = 72$ **26.** $0 = 5x^2 - 245$ **27.** $25x^2 - 16 = 0$

28. $4x^2 + 13 = 49$ **29.** $8x^2 + 10 = 42$ **30.** $36x^2 - 59 = -10$

Solve. Round to the nearest hundredth.

31. $84 - 7x^2 = -22$ **32.** $6x^2 + 44 = 128$ **33.** $13x^2 - 186 = 94$

9-7 Completing the Square

Complete the square for each expression.

34. $x^2 - 14x + \blacksquare$ **35.** $x^2 + 6x + \blacksquare$ **36.** $x^2 - 11x + \blacksquare$

Solve by completing the square.

37. $x^2 + 10x - 11 = 0$ **38.** $x^2 - 24x + 63 = 0$ **39.** $2x^2 - 6x = 20$

40. $3x^2 + 4x + 4 = 3$ **41.** $4x^2 - 12 = 0$ **42.** $x^2 - 2x = 2$

Algebra 1

43. The area of a rectangle is given by $A = x^2 + 4x - 5$. Find the expressions for possible lengths and widths of the rectangle.

9-8 The Quadratic Formula

Solve using the Quadratic Formula. Round your answer to the nearest hundredth.

44. $2x^2 - 4x - 3 = 0$ **45.** $4x^2 + 7x + 2 = 0$ **46.** $8x^2 + 10x - 33 = 0$

47. $x^2 + 2x = 1$ **48.** $2x^2 = 1 - 5x$ **49.** $x(x - 2) = 4$

9-9 The Discriminant

Find the number of solutions of each equation using the discriminant.

50. $14x^2 - 19x - 40 = 0$ **51.** $10x^2 - 9x + 6 = 0$ **52.** $-3x^2 = 18x + 27$

53. $x^2 - 16x = -64$ **54.** $3x^2 = -2x - 5$ **55.** $2x^2 - 5x - 12 = 0$

Algebra 1

Big Ideas

Answer these questions to summarize the important concepts from Chapter 9 in your own words.

1. Explain how to find the axis of symmetry of a parabola that opens upward or downward by using zeros.

2. Explain how to find the vertex of a parabola that opens upward or downward.

3. What are the steps of solving a quadratic equation by factoring?

4. What are the steps for solving a quadratic equation by completing the square?

For more review of Chapter 9:

- Complete the Chapter 9 Study Guide and Review on pages 612–615 of your textbook.

- Complete the Ready to Go On quizzes on pages 567 and 611 of your textbook.

Algebra 1

This table contains important vocabulary terms from Chapter 10. As you work through the chapter, fill in the page number, definition, and a clarifying example for each term.

Term	Page	Definition	Clarifying Example
asymptote			
discontinuous function			
excluded value			
extraneous solution			
inverse variation			

Algebra 1

Inverse Variation

Lesson Objectives

Identify, write, and graph inverse variations

Vocabulary

inverse variation (p. 627): _____

_____

Key Concepts

Inverse Variations (p. 627):

WORDS	NUMBERS	ALGEBRA

Product Rule for Inverse Variation (p. 629):

Think and Discuss (p. 630)

Get Organized In each box, write an example of the parts of the given inverse variation.

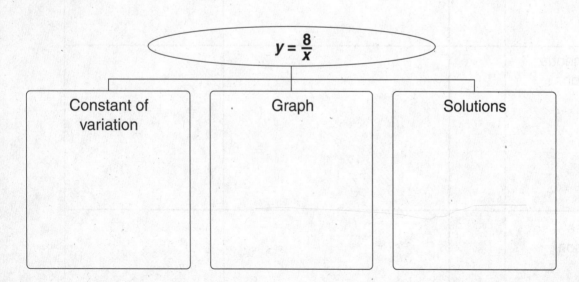

Algebra 1

Rational Functions

LESSON 10-2

Lesson Objectives

Identify excluded values of rational functions; graph rational functions

Vocabulary

rational function (p. 634): _____

_____

excluded value (p. 634): _____

_____

discontinuous function (p. 634): _____

_____

asymptote (p. 634): _____

_____

Key Concepts

Identifying Asymptotes (p. 635):

WORDS	EXAMPLES	

Types of Functions

LINEAR FUNCTIONS

$$y = my + b$$

- Graph is a straight line.
- m is the slope. When $m = 0$, the graph is a horizontal line.
- When $m < 0$, the graph slopes down from left to right.
- When $m > 0$, the graph slopes up from left to right.
- b is the y-intercept.

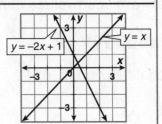

QUADRATIC FUNCTIONS

$$y = ax^2 + bx + c, \, a \neq 0$$

- Graph is a parabola.
- When $a > 0$, the parabola opens up.
- When $a < 0$, the parabola opens down.
- The axis of symmetry is the vertical line $x = -\dfrac{b}{2a}$.
- The function has a maximum or minimum value at the vertex.

RATIONAL FUNCTIONS OF THE FORM $y = \dfrac{a}{x - b} + c$

$$y = \dfrac{1}{x - b} + c$$

- Graph is discontinuous.
- b is an excluded value; $x = b$ is the vertical asymptote.
- $y = c$ is the horizontal asymptote.

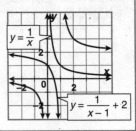

Algebra 1

Think and Discuss (p. 638)

Get Organized In each box, find the asymptotes for the given rations function.

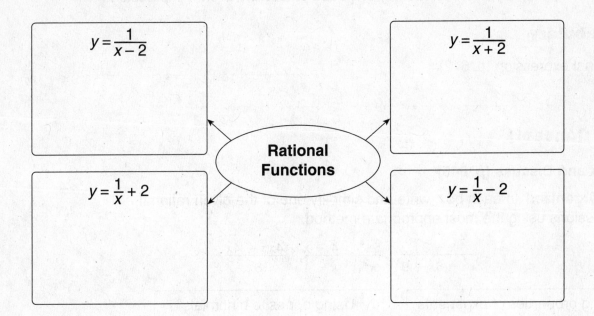

$$y = \frac{1}{x - 2}$$

$$y = \frac{1}{x + 2}$$

Rational Functions

$$y = \frac{1}{x} + 2$$

$$y = \frac{1}{x} - 2$$

Algebra 1

Simplifying Rational Expressions

LESSON 10-3

Lesson Objectives

Simplify rational expressions; Identify excluded values or rational expressions

Vocabulary

rational expression (p. 642): _____

_____

Key Concepts

Think and Discuss (p. 645)

Get Organized In each box, write and simplify one of the given rational expressions using the most appropriate method.

$$\frac{x-3}{x^2-6x+9}, \quad \frac{5x^4}{x^2}, \quad \frac{4-x}{x-4}, \quad \frac{4x^2-4x}{8x}$$

Using properties of exponents	Using opposite binomials

Ways of Simplifying Rational Expressions

Factoring the numerator	Factoring the denominator

Algebra 1

LESSON 10-4 Multiplying and Dividing Rational Expressions

Lesson Objectives

Multiply and divide rational expressions

Key Concepts

Multiplying Rational Expressions (p. 652):

Dividing Rational Expressions (p. 654):

Think and Discuss (p. 655)

Get Organized In each box, describe how to perform the operation with rational expressions.

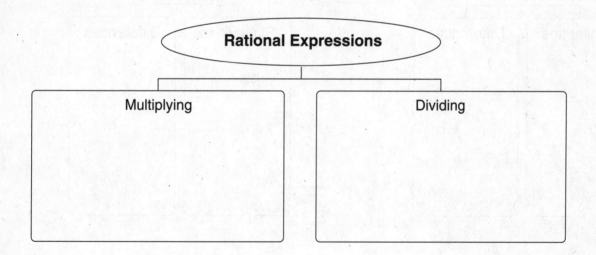

Rational Expressions

Multiplying

Dividing

Algebra 1

LESSON 10-5 Adding and Subtracting Rational Expressions

Lesson Objectives

Add and subtract rational expression with like denominators; Add and subtract rational expressions with unlike denominators

Key Concepts

Adding Rational Expressions with Like Denominators (p. 659):

Think and Discuss (p. 662)

Get Organized In each box, compare and contrast operations with fractions and rational numbers.

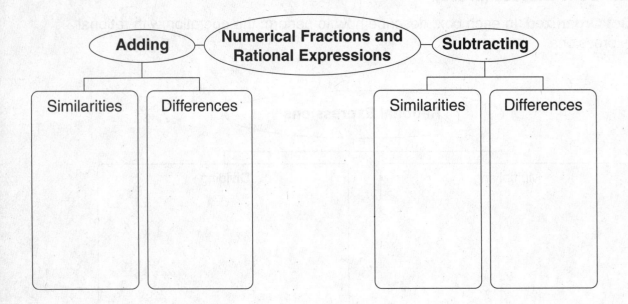

Algebra 1

LESSON 10-6

Dividing Polynomials

Lesson Objectives

Divide a polynomial by a monomial or binomial

Key Concepts

Dividing Polynomials (p. 667):

	WORDS	NUMBERS	ALGEBRA
Step 1			
Step 2			
Step 3			

Think and Discuss (p. 671)

Get Organized In each box, show an example.

```
        ┌──────────────────┐
        │   Long Division  │
        └──────────────────┘
           │            │
┌────────────────┐  ┌────────────────┐
│  Polynomials   │  │  Whole numbers │
│                │  │                │
│                │  │                │
│                │  │                │
└────────────────┘  └────────────────┘
```

151

Algebra 1

LESSON 10-7

Solving Rational Equations

Lesson Objectives

Solve rational equations; Identify extraneous solutions

Vocabulary

rational equation (p. 674): _____

_____

extraneous solution (p. 675): _____

_____

Key Concepts

Think and Discuss (p. 676)

Get Organized In each box, write the solution and check.

```
         ┌─────────────────────────────────┐
         │   Solving Rational Equations    │
         └─────────────────────────────────┘
              │                    │
```

Solve by using cross products.	Solve by using the LCD.
$\dfrac{3}{x} = \dfrac{2}{x+1}$	$\dfrac{7}{x-1} - \dfrac{4}{x-1} = \dfrac{6}{x}$

Algebra 1

Applying Rational Equations

Lesson Objectives

Use rational equations to solve application problems

Key Concepts

Think and Discuss (p. 681)

Get Organized In each box, write an example of each type of application and its solution.

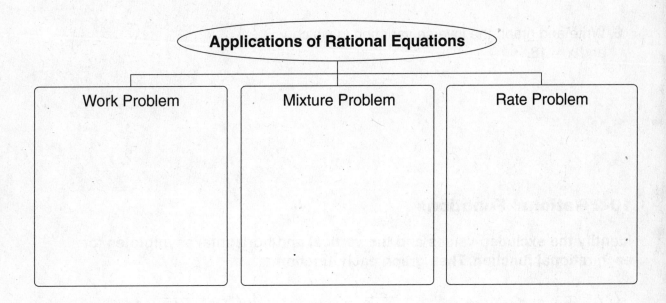

Applications of Rational Equations

Work Problem	Mixture Problem	Rate Problem

Algebra 1

10-1 Inverse Variation

Tell whether each relationship is an inverse variation. Explain.

1.

x	−8	−6	−4
y	−2	−3	−4

2. $y = \dfrac{x}{4}$ 3. $y = \dfrac{4}{x}$ 4. $xy = -4$ 5. $x + y = -4$

6. Write and graph the inverse variation in which $y = \dfrac{1}{2}$ and $x = 18$.

10-2 Rational Functions

Identify the excluded values and the vertical and horizontal asymptotes for each rational function. Then graph each function.

7. $y = -\dfrac{3}{x}$ 8. $y = \dfrac{5}{x + 3}$ 9. $y = \dfrac{5}{2x - 10} + 1$

Algebra 1

10-3 Simplifying Rational Expressions

Simplify each rational expression, if possible. Identify any excluded values.

10. $\dfrac{8x^4}{2x^5}$

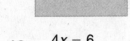

11. $\dfrac{12x - 6}{14x - 7}$

12. $\dfrac{8 - x}{x^2 - 7x - 8}$

13. $\dfrac{4x - 6}{2x^2 - x - 3}$

14. $\dfrac{x^2 + 4x}{x^2 - 16}$

15. $\dfrac{4x^2 + 3x - 10}{25 - 16x^2}$

10-4 Multiplying and Dividing Rational Expressions

Multiply or divide. Simplify your answer.

16. $\dfrac{7x^2}{3} \cdot \dfrac{9}{14x}$

17. $\dfrac{9x^2}{x^2 + 12x + 36} \div \dfrac{12x}{x^2 + 6x}$

18. $\dfrac{x^2 + 2x - 15}{x^2 - 4x - 45} \div \dfrac{x^2 + x - 12}{x^2 - 5x - 36}$

19. $\dfrac{25x^2 - 20x + 4}{x^2 - 1} \cdot \dfrac{x + 1}{10x - 4}$

10-5 Adding and Subtracting Rational Expressions

Add or subtract. Simplify your answer.

20. $\dfrac{y^2}{y - 1} - \dfrac{1}{y - 1}$

21. $\dfrac{10x}{5x - 2} + \dfrac{7x - 2}{5x - 2}$

22. $\dfrac{8}{y^2 - 4y} + \dfrac{2}{y}$

23. $\dfrac{x}{x^2 + x - 2} - \dfrac{1}{x + 2}$

24. $\dfrac{x}{x^2 - 5x + 6} - \dfrac{3}{x - 3}$

25. $\dfrac{1}{x + y} + \dfrac{3x - 3y}{x^2 - y^2}$

Algebra 1

10-6 Dividing Polynomials

Divide. Check your answer.

26. $(21x^3 - 35x^2) \div 7x$ **27.** $(8x^4 - 3x^3) \div x^2$ **28.** $(25x^5 + 15x^4 - 5x^2) \div 5x^2$

Divide using long division.

29. $(x^2 + 9x + 14) \div (x + 7)$ **30.** $(x^2 - 9x - 10) \div (x + 1)$

31. $(3x^3 - 5x^2 + 10x - 3) \div (3x + 1)$

10-7 Solving Rational Equations

Solve. Check your answer.

32. $\dfrac{x - 1}{15} = \dfrac{2}{5}$ **33.** $x + 1 = \dfrac{72}{x}$ **34.** $\dfrac{10}{x(x - 2)} + \dfrac{4}{x} = \dfrac{5}{x - 2}$

10-8 Applying Rational Equations

30. Don can stock shelves in 5 hours. It takes Kim 3 hours to stock the same shelves. How long will it take them to stock the shelves if they work together?

31. Bea and Roberto were practicing for a long-distance boat race. Bea started first and rowed at a rate of 12 km/h. One hour later Roberto left from the same point and rowed in the same direction at a rate of 16 km/h. How many hours did Roberto row before he caught up with Bea?

Algebra 1

Big Ideas

Answer these questions to summarize the important concepts from Chapter 10 in your own words.

1. Explain why $y = \dfrac{1}{x - 3}$ has an asymptote at $x = 3$.

2. When is a rational expression in simplest form?

3. What are the steps for adding or subtracting rational expressions?

4. What are the steps for using long division to divide a polynomial by a binomial?

For more review of Chapter 10:

- Complete the Chapter 10 Study Guide and Review on pages 686–689 of your textbook.

- Compete the Ready to Go On quizzes on pages 651 and 685 of your textbook.

Algebra 1

This table contains important vocabulary terms from Chapter 11. As you work through the chapter, fill in the page number, definition, and a clarifying example for each term.

Term	Page	Definition	Clarifying Example
common ratio			
exponential function			
geometric sequence			
like radicals			
radical equation			
radical expression			
radicand			
square root function			

Algebra 1

Square-Root Functions

Lesson Objectives

Identify square-root functions and their domains; Graph square-root functions

Vocabulary

square-root function (p. 700) _____

_____

Key Concepts

Square-Root Function (p. 700):

WORDS	EXAMPLES	NONEXAMPLES

Think and Discuss (p. 702)

Get Organized In each box, graph the function and give its domain.

Square-Root Functions

$y = \sqrt{x}$	$y = \sqrt{x} + 5$	$y = \sqrt{x + 5}$	$y = \sqrt{5x}$

Algebra 1

Radical Expressions

Lesson Objectives

Simplify radical expressions

Vocabulary

radical expression (p. 705) _____

_____

radicand (p. 705) _____

Key Concepts

Simplest Form of a Square-Root Expression (p. 705):

Product Property of Square Roots (p. 706):

WORDS	NUMBERS	ALGEBRA

Quotient Property of Square Roots (p. 706):

WORDS	NUMBERS	ALGEBRA

Algebra 1

Think and Discuss (p. 708)

Get Organized

In each box, write the property and give an example.

	Product Property of Square Roots	Quotient Property of Square Roots
Words		
Example		

Algebra 1

LESSON 11-3

Adding and Subtracting Radical Expressions

Know it!
Note

Lesson Objectives

Add and subtract radical expressions

Vocabulary

like radicals (p. 711) _____

_____

Key Concepts

Think and Discuss (p. 713)

Get Organized Complete the graphic organizer.

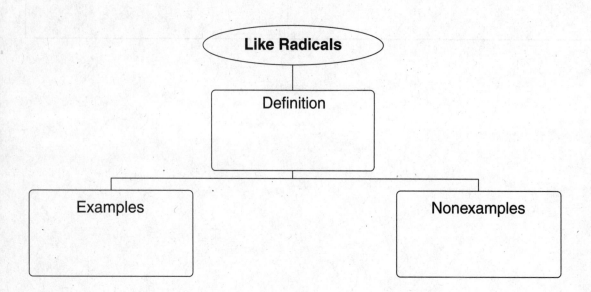

Multiplying and Dividing Radical Expressions

LESSON 11-4

Know it!
Note

Lesson Objectives

Multiply and divide radical expression; Rationalize denominators

Key Concepts

Think and Discuss (p. 718)

Get Organized In each box, give an example and show how to simplify it.

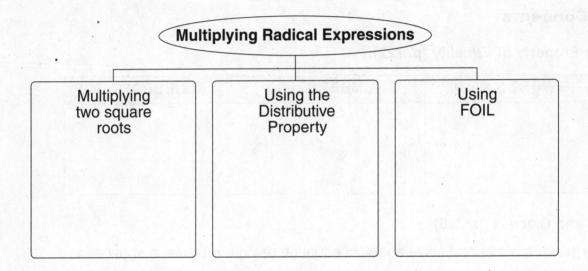

Multiplying Radical Expressions

| Multiplying two square roots | Using the Distributive Property | Using FOIL |

Algebra 1

Solving Radical Equations

LESSON
11-5

Lesson Objectives

Solve radical equations

Vocabulary

radical equation (p. 722) _____

_____

Key Concepts

Power Property of Equality (p. 722):

WORDS	NUMBERS	ALGEBRA

Think and Discuss (p. 726)

Get Organized Write and solve a radical equation using the boxes to show each step.

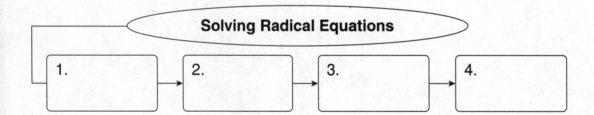

LESSON 11-6 **Geometric Sequences**

Lesson Objectives

Recognize and extend geometric sequences; Find the *n*th term of a geometric sequence

Vocabulary

geometric sequence (p. 732) _____

_____

common ratio (p. 732) _____

_____

Key Concepts

Finding the *n*th Term of a Geometric Sequence (p. 733)

| |
| |
| |
| |

Think and Discuss (p. 734)

Get Organized In each box, write a way to represent the geometric sequence.

Ways to Represent Geometric
Sequence 1, 2, 3, 4, 8, ...

Table	Formula	Words

Exponential Functions

Lesson Objectives

Evaluate exponential functions; Identify and graph exponential functions

Vocabulary

exponential function (p. 738) _____

_____

Key Concepts

Exponential Functions (p. 738):

Graphs of Exponential Functions (p. 741)

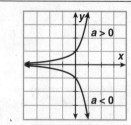	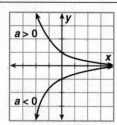
For $y = ab^x$, if $b > 1$, then the graph will have one of these shapes.	For $y = ab^x$, if $0 < b < 1$, then the graph will have one of these shapes.

Think and Discuss (p. 741)

Get Organized In each box, give an example of an appropriate exponential function and sketch its graph.

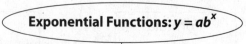

Exponential Functions: $y = ab^x$

$a > 0, b > 1$:	$a < 0, b > 1$:	$a > 0, 0 < b < 1$:	$a < 0, 0 < b < 1$:

Algebra 1

Exponential Growth and Decay

LESSON
11-8

Lesson Objectives

Solve problems involving exponential growth and decay

Vocabulary

exponential growth (p. 747) _____

_____

compound interest (p. 748) _____

_____

exponential decay (p. 749) _____

_____

half-life (p. 749) _____

_____

Key Concepts

Exponential Growth (p. 747):

Compound Interest (p. 748):

Algebra 1

Exponential Decay (p. 749):

Half-life (p. 749):

Think and Discuss (p. 750)

Get Organized Complete the graphic organizer.

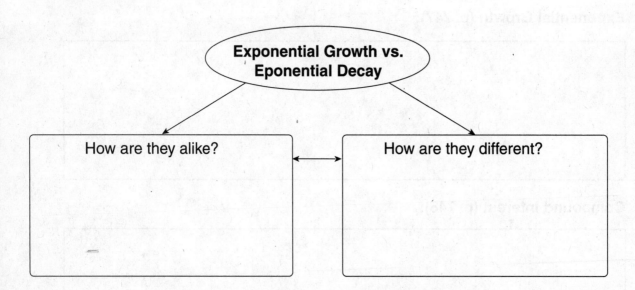

Exponential Growth vs. Eponential Decay

How are they alike?

How are they different?

Algebra 1

Linear, Quadratic, and Exponential Models

Lesson Objectives

Compare linear, quadratic, and exponential models; Given a set of data, decide which type of function models the data and write an equation to describe the function

Key Concepts

General Forms of Functions (p. 757):

LINEAR	QUADRATIC	EXPONENTIAL

Think and Discuss (p. 758)

Get Organized In each box, list some characteristics and sketch a graph of each type of model.

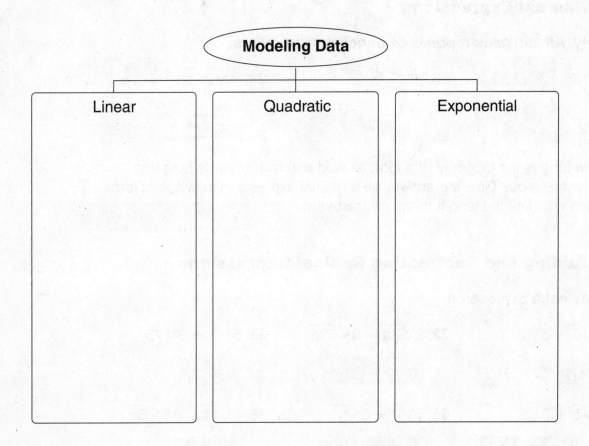

Chapter Review

11-1 Square-Root Functions

Find the domain of each square-root function.

19. $y = \sqrt{x + 2} - 1$

20. $y = \sqrt{4x - 1}$

21. $y = \sqrt{2(x - 4)} + 3$

Graph each square-root function.

22. $y = \sqrt{x + 3} - 2$

23. $y = \frac{1}{4}\sqrt{x + 2}$

11-2 Radical Expressions

Simplify. All variables represent nonnegative numbers.

24. $\sqrt{108}$

25. $\sqrt{\dfrac{324}{4}}$

26. $-\sqrt{25a^4 b^6}$

27. $\sqrt{\dfrac{72}{49}}$

28. $\sqrt{\dfrac{16a^6}{b^4}}$

29. $\sqrt{\dfrac{98a^2 b^4}{48b^2}}$

30. How long is the diagonal of a football field that is 100 yards long and 50 yards wide? Give the answer as a radical expression in simplest form. Then estimate the length to the nearest yard.

11-3 Adding and Subtracting Radical Expressions

Simplify each expression.

31. $2\sqrt{3} + 5\sqrt{3}$

32. $2\sqrt{7a} + 5\sqrt{63a}$

33. $5\sqrt{3} + 2\sqrt{75}$

34. $4\sqrt{5} + 3\sqrt{7}$

35. $5\sqrt{8} - 3\sqrt{18} + \sqrt{3}$

36. $2\sqrt{20x} + 3\sqrt{5x}$

Algebra 1

11-4 Multiplying and Dividing Radical Expressions

Multiply. Write each product in simplest form.

37. $\sqrt{3}\sqrt{5}$

38. $2\sqrt{18}(3\sqrt{8})$

39. $2\sqrt{6}(3\sqrt{7})$

40. $(2\sqrt{5})^2$

41. $(6 - \sqrt{2})(6 + \sqrt{2})$

42. $(\sqrt{a} - 5)(3\sqrt{a} + 7)$

Simplify each quotient.

43. $\dfrac{\sqrt{6}}{\sqrt{3}}$

44. $\dfrac{4}{2\sqrt{3}}$

45. $\dfrac{\sqrt{50}}{\sqrt{y^2}}$

46. $\dfrac{6\sqrt{10}}{8\sqrt{2}}$

47. $\dfrac{-12\sqrt{24}}{3\sqrt{2}}$

48. $\dfrac{2\sqrt{x}}{\sqrt{x} + \sqrt{y}}$

11-5 Solving Radical Equations

Solve each equation. Check your answer.

49. $\sqrt{x} = 5$

50. $\sqrt{2x} - 4 = 2$

51. $\sqrt{x + 7} = 10$

52. $\dfrac{\sqrt{x}}{4} = 5$

53. $\sqrt{x + 5} - \sqrt{x} = 1$

54. $\sqrt{7 - x} + \sqrt{x + 11} = 6$

55. A rectangle has an area of 72 m². Its length is 9 m, and its width is $(\sqrt{x} - 20)$ m. What is the value of x?

11-6 Geometric Sequences

Find the next three terms in each geometric sequence.

1. 16, −8, 4, −2, 1, . . .   **2.** 0.01, 0.06, 0.36, 2.16, . . .   **3.** 1458, 486, 162, 54, . . .

4. What is the 8th term of the geometric sequence 1, 3, 9, 27, . . .?

5. The first term of a geometric sequence is 77, and the common ratio is 0.7. What is the 7th term of the sequence?

6. The ninth term of a geometric sequence is −3. The common ratio is −1. Find the first term of the sequence.

11-7 Exponential Functions

7. The function $f(x) = 2500(0.5)^x$, where x is the time in years, models the number of gaming systems sold to students at a middle school. How many gaming systems will be sold in 4 years?

Graph each exponential function.

8. $y = 6(2)^x$ **9.** $y = -5(0.5)^x$ **10.** $y = -\left(1\frac{1}{2}\right)^x$

Algebra 1

11-8 Exponential Growth and Decay

Write a function to model each situation. Then find the value of the function after the given amount of time.

11. Ed invested $5000 for college tuition and he expects to receive 5% interest annually; 5 years.

12. A $1600 computer is losing value at a rate of 10% per year; 3 years.

13. $3500 is invested at a rate of 5.5% compounded quarterly; 4 years.

14. Francium-233 has a half-life of approximately 22 minutes. Find the amount of francium-233 left from an 88-gram sample after 54 minutes.

11-9 Linear, Quadratic, and Exponential Models

Look for a pattern in each data set to determine which kind of model best describes the data.

15. {(−20, 17), (−10, 12), (0, 7), (10, 2), (20, −3)}

16. {(−7, 5), (−6, −4), (−5, −7), (−4, −4), (−3, 5)}

Graph each data set. Which kind of model best describes the data?

17. {(−2, −12), (2, 2), (6, 8), (10, 6), (14, −4)}

18. {(−1, 0.125), (0, 0.25), (1, 0.5), (2, 1), (4, 4)}

Algebra 1

Big Ideas

Answer these questions to summarize the important concepts from Chapter 11 in your own words.

1. Explain the difference between the graphs $f(x) = \sqrt{x} + 4$ and $f(x) = \sqrt{x + 4}$.

2. Explain how you know when a square-root expression is in simplest form.

3. Explain how to solve the equation $\sqrt{x} - 5 = 20$.

4. Explain the difference between exponential growth and exponential decay.

5. When the independent variable changes by a constant amount, what are the characteristics of linear functions, quadratic functions, and exponential functions?

For more review of Chapter 11:

• Complete the Chapter 11 Study Guide and Review on pages 764–767.

• Complete the Ready to Go On quizzes on pages 731 and 763.

Algebra 1